J
B
JAC   Pflueger, Lynda
       Stonewall Jackson:
       Confederate General

DISCARD

DATE DUE

DE 27 '99			

J
BIO
JAC

HISTORICAL AMERICAN BIOGRAPHIES

STONEWALL JACKSON

Confederate General

Lynda Pflueger

Enslow Publishers, Inc.

44 Fadem Road   PO Box 38
Box 699   Aldershot
Springfield, NJ 07081 Hants GU12 6BP
USA   UK

Dedication:
to Jon and Karen for their loving support.

Library of Congress Cataloging-in-Publication Data

Pflueger, Lynda.
    Stonewall Jackson : Confederate general / Lynda Pflueger.
       p. cm. — (Historical American biographies)
    Includes bibliographical references and index.
    Summary: A biography of the Confederate general who gained the
nickname Stonewall for his stand at the first battle of Bull Run during
the Civil War.
    ISBN 0-89490-781-6
    1. Jackson, Stonewall, 1824–1863—Juvenile literature. 2. Generals—
Confederate States of America—Biography—Juvenile literature.
3.Confederate States of America. Army—Biography—Juvenile literature.
[1. Jackson, Stonewall, 1824–1863. 2. Generals. 3. United States—
History—Civil War, 1861–1865.] I. Title. II. Series.
E467.1. J15P48 1997
973.7'092—dc20
  [B]
                                     96-8827
                                        CIP
                                        AC

Printed in the United States of America

10 9 8 7 6 5 4 3 2 1

Illustration Credits: Chicago Historical Society, p. 62; Stephen Klimek,
p. 100; Gary Koellhoffer, p. 87; Library of Congress, pp. 8, 10, 95;
Massachusetts Commandery, Military Order of the Loyal Legion and the
US Army Military History Institute, pp. 36, 70, 98; Kristin McCarthy,
p. 107; National Archives, pp. 46, 59, 66, 74, 76, 109; United States
Military Academy, pp. 26, 30; Valentine Museum, p. 56; Virginia
Military Institute, pp. 44, 115; West Virginia State Archives, pp. 17, 83,
105.

Cover Illustrations: ©1996 Carolyn J. Yaschur (background); West
Virginia State Archives (inset).

CONTENTS

1

THEY CALLED HIM "STONEWALL"

The first major battle of the Civil War took place in July of 1861 beside a small stream called Bull Run near Manassas Junction, Virginia. During the battle, one man stood out from all the rest, General Thomas Jackson, a former professor at the Virginia Military Institute. Jackson placed his men in a strategic position on Henry House Hill, where they valiantly stood their ground. By refusing to give way, they turned the battle around.

In the South, battles were named after towns, and in the North after the nearest landmark, such as a river or stream. Therefore, in the South this battle was called the Battle of Manassas and in the North, the Battle of Bull Run.

Forward to Richmond

The confrontation began on July 18, when the Union Army, made up of thirty-seven thousand volunteers, crossed the Potomac River and marched into Virginia.[1] Under the command of General Irvin McDowell they set out to destroy the railroad at Manassas Junction and then move on to capture Richmond, the capital of the Confederate States of America.

The Southern Army knew McDowell was coming. Mrs. Rose O'Neal Greenhow, a Washington socialite and Confederate spy, sent word to General Pierre G. T. Beauregard. Her coded message was hidden in a small box and then tucked into the hair of a young Southern sympathizer. The message read, "McDowell has certainly been ordered to advance on the sixteenth."[2] It was signed "R.O.G."

To block the invasion General Beauregard sent his troops north to form an eight-mile line along Bull Run. He also asked the Confederate government in Richmond to send him reinforcements. General Joseph E. Johnston's army in the Shenandoah Valley was ordered to Manassas. One of the first brigades to depart from the Valley was General Thomas Jackson's First Brigade of Virginia. On the morning of July 18, they prepared three days worth of

Rose O'Neal Greenhow was an attractive widow with many influential friends in Washington. After her husband's death she used her numerous political connections to obtain important government jobs or promotions for anyone who would "contribute to her upkeep."[3] Shortly after the Civil War began she was recruited to spy for the Confederacy.

In time the Federal Secret Service became suspicious of Rose's activities. When they searched her home they found alphabets, numbers, ciphers, and various other tools for creating coded messages. She was eventually arrested and listed in the prison record book as "a dangerous, skillful spy."[4]

rations, packed their gear, and began their march. Fifteen hundred strong, they were eager for action.

Shortly after their march began, Jackson called his men to a halt and read their orders aloud. "Our gallant army under General Beauregard is now attacked by overwhelming numbers. The Commanding General hopes that his troops will step out like men, and make a forced march to save the country."[5] The men shouted wildly and continued on their march with greater determination.

By dusk they reached the Shenandoah River and waded through the waist-deep water while holding their muskets high over their heads. By two o'clock in the morning they could go on no further. Jackson ordered them to bivouac—sleep out on the mountainside. Exhausted, they lay down beside the trees and boulders and slept. When dawn broke the following morning, they were on their way again. They marched ten miles south to Piedmont, a station on the Manassas Gap Railroad, where railroad cars waited to take them to Manassas.

When Jackson reported to General Beauregard, he was ordered to position his men in a pine grove near Mitchell's Ford. As they approached their assigned

This peaceful little stream, called Bull Run, was the site of two major battles during the Civil War.

position they passed fresh graves—evidence of the previous day's battle. They spent an uneasy night waiting for the battle to begin. On Sunday, July 21, at 6:30 A.M., they were awakened by the roar of cannons.

Henry House Hill

Quickly they formed a battle line in support of General James Longstreet's brigade. The battle raged for hours, and the Confederate troops began to lose ground. Near mid-morning a courier raced to Jackson with urgent orders to move his men to the crest of Henry House Hill and support the Confederate battle line to their left.

In the summer heat they marched at double time through the woods and across the fields to their new position. Jackson surveyed the scene and placed his artillery on the ridge that formed a crescent around the top of the hill. Behind the ridge, a thick forest provided protection for his men.

For several hours they lay on the ground behind the artillery waiting for the battle to come to them. Shells exploded over their heads, and they watched as the wounded men from other brigades limped or crawled over the hill and through their lines. The battle moved closer and closer. Soon shells exploded near their positions. Many of the men said their prayers aloud. Jackson calmly walked his horse back and forth in front of his men. His calm demeanor and soothing words, "Steady, men! steady! all's well!"[6] helped calm the soldiers' nerves. One of his men later said that Jackson "rode about in that shower of death as calmly as a farmer about his farm when the seasons are good."[7]

Around noon Brigadier General Barnard Bee from South Carolina rode up to Jackson to announce that his men were falling back, and the enemy would soon be upon them. Jackson firmly replied, "Then, sir, we will give them the bayonet."[8] He ordered his men into position.

The Henry House was destroyed during the first Battle of Bull Run. The owner of the house, eighty-year-old Judith Henry, became the first casualty of the Civil War when a cannon shell tore through her bedroom wall and exploded.

Jackson "Standing Like a Stone Wall"

Bee rode back to his retreating men and urged them to stand their ground. "Look! There is Jackson standing like a stone wall! Rally behind the Virginians!"[9]

It was the turning point of the battle. The Confederate forces rallied around Jackson's Virginia brigade and stood their ground. The battle continued for several hours. At one point it appeared that Union troops would penetrate their line. An officer from the 33rd Virginia Regiment rushed to Jackson. "General! The day is going against us."[10]

"If you think so, sir," he replied, "you had better not say anything about it."[11]

Jackson ordered his men to stand up. "We'll charge them now and drive them to Washington."[12] Like a man, "determined to conquer or die,"

A large group of spectators rode out from Washington to see the battle. They sat out on the grass at the edge of the battlefield with their picnic baskets and waited to see the Confederate rebels get the whipping they thought they deserved. The picnic ended when the defeated Union troops began to retreat. A great panic set in, and frightened civilians and soldiers flooded the road back to Washington.

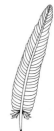

Jackson yelled, "Reserve your fire until they come within fifty yards, then fire and give them the bayonet; and, when you charge, yell like furies!"[13]

They charged, striking the Union's center line and battered away at them until finally their battle lines gave way. The Union soldiers turned and ran toward Bull Run. They did not stop running until they crossed the Potomac and reached Washington thirty miles away.

Of the 28,452 Union soldiers who fought in the battle, 481 were killed, 1,011 were wounded, and 1,216 were missing. The combined Confederate forces totaled 32,232 men, and 387 were killed, 1,582 were wounded, and 12 were missing.[14] Jackson's First Brigade suffered the heaviest losses— 119 of his men were killed and 442 were wounded.[15]

Jackson was wounded during the battle. While a physician set the broken bone in his middle finger, he proclaimed, "We have whipped them! They ran like sheep! Give me 10,000 men and I will take Washington City tomorrow."[16]

That day the South won a decisive victory and a new hero was born. Thomas Jackson became known as "Stonewall" Jackson, and throughout the North and the South his victories were proclaimed. The headline of one Richmond newspaper read: "Glorious old Stonewall is fast becoming a hero of the war."[17] In the North, mothers sometimes threatened their naughty children with "Be good or Stonewall will get you!"[18]

2

THE ORPHAN

Thomas Jackson was the third child of Judith Beckworth Neale, born on February 29, 1798, and Jonathan Jackson, born on September 25, 1790. His mother, whom everyone called Julia, was a well-educated gray-eyed beauty. She was the third child in a family of eleven children. Thomas's father, Jonathan, also came from a large family. He was the third child in a family of fifteen and was educated at the Randolph Academy in Clarksburg and the Old Male Academy in Parkersburg. Then he studied law in the office of Congressman John George Jackson, his cousin.

Julia Neale and Jonathan Jackson were childhood friends and classmates. They married on September 28, 1817. They lived in a small three-room brick house across the street from the courthouse where Jonathan Jackson practiced law. Two years after their marriage, their first child, Elizabeth, was born in March of 1819. In January of 1821 their second child, Warren, was born.

Thomas Jackson was born around midnight on the night of January 20, 1824, in Clarksburg, Virginia. The doctor who delivered him, Dr. James McCally, thought he arrived before midnight on the twentieth. Since Thomas's family lost the official record of his birth, no one knows for sure whether he was born on the twentieth or the twenty-first. His mother named Thomas after her father, Thomas Neale, but gave him no middle name.

Tom, as his family called him, was two years old when his sister, Elizabeth, came down with typhoid fever. Typhoid fever, a highly contagious disease, often wiped out entire families. Due to his wife's advanced pregnancy with their fourth child, Jonathan nursed his daughter by himself. Elizabeth died on March 5, 1826. Shortly after Elizabeth died Jonathan came down with the fever. He died on March 26. The next day Judith Jackson gave birth to their fourth child, Laura Ann.

Unfortunately for his family, Jonathan Jackson had been a gambler and left them penniless. Alone with a baby and two small children, Judith Jackson did what she could to support her family. She took in sewing and ran a school in her home.

After nearly four years of widowhood, she married another lawyer, Blake Woodson. Shortly after their marriage, Woodson was appointed to the post of clerk in the new county of Fayette, Virginia, and they moved to Ansted, 125 miles away. Due to their limited resources, Judith Jackson Woodson found it necessary to send Warren, her eldest son, to live with her brother, Alfred Neale, in Parkersburg. A few months later, she arranged to send Tom, age six, and Laura, age three, to live with their father's family in Jackson's Mill in western Virginia.

Laura did not understand what was going on, but Tom did. When his uncle came to get them, he ran away and hid in the woods. He stayed there until nightfall. When he returned, his mother cried and hugged him. She was relieved that he was safe but encouraged him to go. His uncle promised treats and talked about the great time they would have hunting and fishing. Finally after two days, Tom gave in.

A few months after they arrived at Jackson's Mill, their mother sent for them. Her health had declined rapidly after the birth of her fifth son,

William Wirt Woodson. She knew she was dying and wanted to say good-bye to her children. A trusted family slave, "Uncle" Robinson, quickly took Laura and Tom on horseback to see their mother for the last time.

They arrived in time to receive her dying blessing. Standing beside her bed, they listened to her pleas for God to watch over her family. She died on December 3, 1831. Tom, then seven years old, never forgot his mother's earnest prayers.

Jackson's Mill

The children arrived back at Jackson's Mill and into the care of their paternal grandmother, Elizabeth Jackson. They received a lot of attention from their three unmarried uncles and two aunts. Young Laura charmed her uncles with her pretty face and sweet ways. Tom was a favorite of his Uncle Cummins Jackson.

Cummins Jackson became the head of his family when his father, Edward Jackson, died. He managed the family's farm where they grew crops, raised sheep and horses, and ran a saw mill and grist mill. A grist mill grinds grain into flour. They also owned a small number of slaves who lived in cabins behind the big house. Tom developed a fondness for two of the slaves, old "Uncle" Robinson and "Granny" Nancy Robinson. "Uncle" Robinson was always

doing something to help him. He showed Tom how to make a canoe out of a log and helped him get ready to ride his uncles' horses in races. "Granny" Nancy Robinson was the leader of the slaves and a devout Christian. She preached the Bible to anyone who would listen.

During his youth Tom developed a stomach ailment that plagued him most of his life. The only thing that relieved his indigestion was plenty of fresh air and exercise. Life at Jackson's Mill provided an abundance of both.

Jackson's Mill is located in West Virginia on the Monongahela River where it swerves east and then a quarter of a mile later swings northwest creating a peninsula shaped like a horseshoe.

Tom's grandmother, Elizabeth Jackson, died in August of 1835. This left Laura and Tom in the care of their three bachelor uncles. Many members of the family did not feel this was a good situation, particularly for Laura. They sent her to live with her Aunt Rebecca White near Parkersburg.

A New Home

Shortly after Laura left, Tom's uncles decided he needed a more normal home. They sent him to live with his Aunt Polly Brake, in Harrison County near Clarksburg, Virginia. Things did not work out well for Tom. His Uncle Brake was hard to please and demanded that he do thankless jobs without any rewards. He even made Tom work on Sunday.

Eleven-year-old Tom tried to stick it out but finally gave up and left. He walked fifteen miles to a cousin's home in Clarksburg. After supper his cousin asked him what was wrong. Tom told him, "Uncle Brake and I can't agree; I have quit and shall not go back any more."[1] His cousin tried to persuade Tom that there had been a misunderstanding and he should go back, but Tom could not be reasoned with. He left his cousin's home and spent the night with another relative in Clarksburg. In the morning he was told again that he should go back to his Uncle Brake's. Instead, he walked eighteen miles to Jackson's Mill and to his favorite uncle, Cummins Jackson.

Back to Jackson's Mill

Cummins seemed to understand his nephew's stubbornness and strong sense of fair play. He welcomed him back with open arms. Later Tom wrote that his uncle had provided him with the only real home he had ever known.

Tom worked hard for his uncle. He did whatever farm chores he was asked to do. He rode his uncle's thoroughbred horses in races although he felt and looked awkward on a horse. One of his favorite jobs was shearing the sheep. He would haul the wool to a carding mill and then take it home. There it was spun into yarn, woven into cloth, and made into clothes. For most of his early years he wore homespun clothes.

He also loved to go fishing, and made an agreement with Conrad Kester, the local gunsmith, to provide fresh fish for his table. While on the way to deliver a fish, his neighbor, Colonel John Talbott, stopped him. He complimented Tom on the fine fish he was carrying and asked him how much he would take for it. Tom told him the fish was not for sale, but the colonel tried to haggle. He offered him a dollar and a quarter. Tom replied, "Colonel Talbott, I have an agreement with Mr. Kester to furnish him fish of a certain length for fifty cents each. He has taken some from me a little shorter than that; now he is going to get this big fish for fifty cents."[2]

Tom attended school whenever he could. In the mountain country of Virginia the school term ran for only three months a year. Children attended school between the planting and harvesting seasons. At other times they were needed at home to help their families. According to one of his cousins, Tom was not a brilliant student. "He learned slowly, but what he got in his head he never forgot."[3]

Because he learned slowly, Thomas sometimes studied late into the night. The fireplace provided his only light, so he made an agreement with one of Uncle Cummins's slaves. Thomas would teach him to read and write—at the time this was strictly forbidden—if the slave would provide pine knots to burn in the fireplace. The arrangement worked well until his student learned enough to write himself a pass and run away to Canada by way of the Underground Railroad.

In his youth Tom developed an interest in religion. He was careful not to force his views on other people, but he was always ready to discuss religion when asked. The daughter of the local Methodist minister noted that Tom was a shy boy who would walk three miles just to sit quietly and listen to one of her father's long sermons. For a while Tom thought about becoming a minister, but his lack of education and fear of public speaking discouraged him from doing so.

Warren Jackson Comes to Visit

In the fall of 1836, when Tom was twelve years old, his brother, Warren, came for a visit. Tom idolized his well-educated brother, who taught school in Upshur County. The brothers decided to go visit their sister, Laura, in Parkersburg on the Ohio River. While in Parkersburg they heard rumors about men making their fortunes by cutting down trees on the river islands and selling the wood to steamboats as they passed by. Eager for adventure, they set out to make their fortunes.

A few months later they returned to Parkersburg with only one thing to show for their efforts—new trunks. Since they had to travel home on foot and the trunks were too heavy to carry, they gave them

The Underground Railroad was a secret network of Northerners who opposed slavery. They helped slaves who had escaped from the South make their way north. The operators of the railroad were called "conductors" and their houses "stations." A fugitive slave was passed from station to station until he reached safety in one of the free states or Canada.

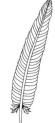

away. Tom gave his trunk to his sister, Laura. Warren gave his to Wirt Woodson, his half brother.

After their adventure, Tom and Warren came down with chills and a fever—which in those days was called "ague." Tom eventually got over his ailment, but three years later Warren died in November 1841 of consumption, now called tuberculosis. It was believed he contracted the disease while working on the river.

Engineering Assistant and Teacher

When Tom returned to Jackson's Mill, he went to work as an engineering assistant with the Parkersburg and Staunton Turnpike Company. They had a contract to build a road that would connect the Shenandoah Valley with the Ohio River. "Problems of engineering and the compass and the level seemed to appeal to him . . . he was described as being one of the best fellows on the job, always doing what he was told and doing it well."[4]

At the end of summer Tom quit his job and went back to school. Friends persuaded him to follow in his brother's footsteps and become a teacher. For three months he taught in a school supported by the Virginia Literary Fund. The more he taught the stronger his desire grew to go to college, where he felt a person could learn "how to work his head."[5]

3

THE CADET

In the spring of 1842 an appointment to the United States Military Academy at West Point became available in the congressional district where Thomas Jackson lived. Eighteen years old and eager to further his education, Thomas applied. The local congressman, Samuel L. Hays, set up an examination to determine the most qualified candidate. At the time, West Point was strictly an engineering school, and a great deal of emphasis was placed on mathematics. One candidate, Gibson J. Butcher, scored the highest on that part of the examination and received the appointment.

Life at West Point did not suit Butcher. After staying a short time he left without informing the superintendent. On his way back home, he stopped at Jackson's Mill and told Thomas and his family what had happened. "After seeing the movements and learning the duties which I had to perform I came to the conclusion that I never could consent to live the life. I did not know as much about the institution when I applied for the appointment as I know now."[1]

Immediately, Thomas began to pursue the appointment again. He asked a friend to tutor him in mathematics and sought out members of the community to support his nomination. One influential friend asked Thomas a rather embarrassing question. Did he "think his educational background good enough to sustain him if he received the appointment?"[2] Boldly he replied, "I am very ignorant but I can make it up in study. I know I have the energy and I think I have the intellect."[3]

Thomas went to Washington to present his case to Congressman Hays. With him he carried five letters. One letter was Butcher's resignation. The other four letters highly praised Jackson's qualifications and contained petitions signed by thirty-one well-known community members. Congressman Hays immediately sent a letter to the secretary of war apologizing for Butcher's resignation and recommending that Thomas Jackson replace him. He also stated that he was "personally and intimately acquainted with young Jackson" and that he had a "good moral character—and an improvable mind."[4]

Arrival at West Point

On June 20, 1842, Thomas arrived at West Point. He was dressed in his best gray homespun clothes, wearing an old felt hat, and carrying his belongings in weather-beaten saddlebags slung over his shoulder. His backwoods appearance did not go unnoticed. Onlookers observed a tall, suntanned young man with blue eyes and wavy brown hair. His head was bent forward and he walked quickly with an awkward gait. One cadet, impressed by his determined look, remarked, "That fellow looks as if he had come to stay."[5]

He reported to the administrative staff office, where he signed his name, Thomas J. Jackson, in the Descriptive List of New Cadets for the year 1842. Prior to entering West Point, Jackson began to use a middle initial. It appears he chose *J* in honor of his father, Jonathan Jackson. From there he went to the quartermaster's office and was issued the minimum equipment he would need: a chair, two blankets, a comforter, an arithmetic text, a slate, a bucket, a tin

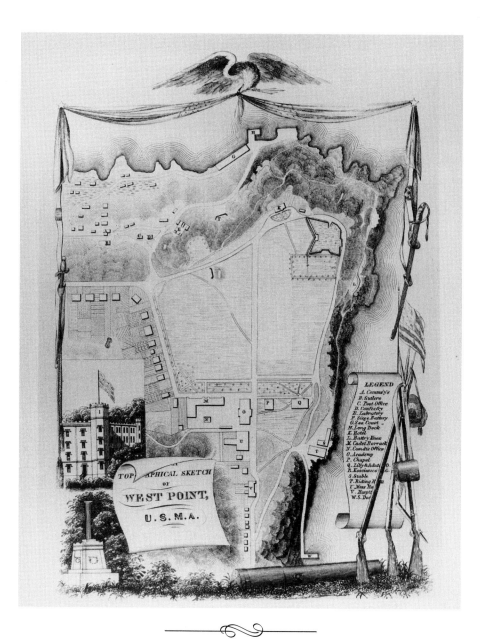

TOPOGRAPHICAL SKETCH
OF
WEST POINT,
U. S. M. A.

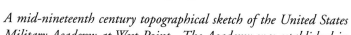

A mid-nineteenth century topographical sketch of the United States Military Academy at West Point. The Academy was established in 1802 to train men to become officers in the United States Army.

cup, a washbasin and soap, stationery, a candle, and a candlestick.[6]

The academy's entrance examinations were given on June 23 through 25. One of Jackson's classmates later remarked, "With his whole soul Jackson was bent upon passing . . . When he went to the blackboard the perspiration was streaming from his face, and during the whole examination his anxiety was painful to witness."[7] At 3:00 P.M. on Saturday, June 25, a list was posted announcing the names of those who had passed the examinations. Thomas J. Jackson's name was on the list.

When the cadets first arrived at West Point, they were housed in tents and taught the basics of military life by upperclassmen, who also impressed upon them their lowly status of "plebe." This was called "beast barracks." Many cadets gave up and went home due to the harassment they received. Jackson's stubbornness and determination got him through.

After beast barracks, cadets were moved into small dormlike rooms in regular barracks. Each room housed four or five cadets, had a bare floor, and was heated by a coal grate. The cadets slept on iron beds. Posted in each room were specific instructions regarding where to keep all clothing and equipment. Cadets bathed once a week and had to obtain permission from the superintendent to bathe more often.

The First Year

During the first year, cadets practiced marching and were drilled in the use of weapons for two or three hours a day. They then spent nine to ten hours in classes or studying. Each class was called a section and consisted of fifteen cadets. Every day cadets recited in their classes and were graded on their progress. Jackson's poor educational background made this difficult for him. When he could not understand a day's lesson, he worked on it until he learned it—no matter how long it took. This put him further and further behind. Often he had to get up in class and admit he came unprepared. His first semester was a painful ordeal.

Determined not to give up, he developed rigid study habits. After taps each evening he would pile coal high in the grate and stretch out on the floor in front of the fire. There he would study his lessons until he mastered them. One of his roommates later remarked he "literally 'burned' knowledge into his brain."[8]

Examinations were held twice a year, and each cadet was graded and ranked within his class. At the end of the first year, out of a class of seventy-two, Thomas ranked fifty-first in general merit, forty-fifth in mathematics, and seventieth in French. His standing in the conduct roll was 38 out of the entire cadet corps of 223. He had only fifteen demerits.

Jackson survived his first year at West Point through sheer willpower. When asked by one of his aunts how he succeeded, Jackson replied, "Aunt, I *studied* and *cried* and *prayed.*"[9]

Rules to Live By

Even with the worst part of his ordeal behind him, Jackson did not slow down his efforts for self-improvement. He began to keep a book of maxims—moral and ethical rules to live by. The maxim that seems to best describe Jackson's years at West Point is: "You may be whatever you resolve to be."[10]

Midway through Jackson's second year at West Point, he wrote a letter to his sister in which he discussed his future plans. He felt there were two courses of action he could take, the "profession of arms" or "that of a civil pursuit, as law."[11] Homesickness seemed to be getting to him. He told her he would remain in the army long enough to distinguish himself and then return home.

At that point Thomas had survived courses in French, English grammar, and mathematics. In the next two years he climbed more academic hurdles and gained competency in chemistry, natural and

Cadets relax under the trees at West Point.

experimental philosophy, engineering, mineralogy and geology, artillery, and infantry tactics.

The most frustrating of all his courses was drawing. The course taught by Robert W. Weir covered lettering, topographical drawing, signs and symbols, drawing the human figure, and painting in oils and watercolors. Many years later in a letter to a friend, Thomas admitted, "My hardest tasks at West Point were the drawing lessons, and I could never do anything in that line to satisfy myself or anyone else."[12]

In his last year at West Point he starred in Reverend Martin P. Parks's ethics class. He ranked fifth in the class, the highest order of merit he achieved in any of his classes. In a letter to his sister, Laura, he described ethics as his favorite course. The subject was closely related to the study of religion, which greatly interested him in later years.

During his years of rigid study, Jackson developed several unusual personal habits. His stomach ailment returned, and he felt that sitting upright without touching the back of a chair while reading or concentrating put less strain on his digestive system. Also, convinced that one of his arms was larger than the other, he made a habit of raising it—straight up in the air—to let his blood run

The West Point class of 1846 supplied the Union Army with fifteen generals and the Confederate Army with nine. A few of the Union generals were: George B. McClellan, Darius N. Couch, and George Stoneman. A few of the Confederate generals were: Thomas J. Jackson, Dabney H. Maury, and Cadmus M. Wilcox. Also attending West Point at the time were: Ulysses S. Grant, Winfield Scott Hancock, William S. Rosecrans, James Longstreet, and Barnard E. Bee.

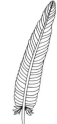

back into his body. Although his odd behavior led to many jokes, Thomas was generally well-liked and respected by his peers.

Possible War with Mexico

Just prior to graduation he wrote to his sister about the possibility of war with Mexico.

> Rumor appears to indicate a rupture between our government and the Mexican. If such should be the case the probability is that I will be ordered to join the army of occupation immediately, and, if so, will hardly see home until after my return, and the next letter that you will receive from me may be dated Texas or Mexico.[13]

At the end of his four years at West Point, Jackson stood in the top third of his graduating class. Out of a class of fifty-nine he ranked seventeenth. His classmates joked that if he attended West Point one more year, he would have been ranked number one in his class.

4

SOLDIER AND TEACHER

On July 1, 1846, Jackson graduated from West Point. He was commissioned a brevet second lieutenant, an honorary rank, in the United States Army and assigned to the artillery division. After graduation he spent two weeks visiting his sister, Laura, in Beverly, Virginia, and a short time with his family in Jackson's Mill. Then he received orders to report to Captain Francis Taylor's Company K in New York. Shortly after he arrived, Company K left for Mexico.

The United States and Mexico were in the middle of a land dispute. During the first part of the nineteenth century, many Americans migrated into lands that Mexico claimed. Texas was the most heavily populated of these areas. By 1834 over thirty thousand Americans lived there.[1]

Although the American settlers agreed to convert to Catholicism and obey Mexican laws, few followed through with their promises. Many of the settlers were from the South and brought their slaves with them. The Mexicans strongly opposed slavery and resented the *Anglos*, as they called the Americans, for not obeying their laws.

This situation frustrated Mexican leaders, but for many years they did nothing. Leadership in Mexico changed often, and the Anglo settlements were located over eight hundred miles from the Mexican capital, Mexico City. Between Mexico City and the settlements lay rugged mountain ranges, deserts, and several dozen rivers. When General Antonio Lopez de Santa Anna became the leader of Mexico, he sent troops to reinforce the military outposts on the Rio Grande River in southern Texas. He hoped that by showing force he could make the Texans conform. His strategy backfired, and the angry Texans rebelled.

Texas

Eventually Texas won its battle for independence from Mexico, and a movement began to add Texas to the United States. Southern politicians favored adding Texas to the Union because it was a way of spreading the institution of slavery. Many Northerners feared that adding another slave state would give the South control over Congress.

The annexation debate raged on until 1844, when James K. Polk was elected president of the United States. He believed in the country's Manifest Destiny—the right to expand her territories across northern America all the way to the Pacific Ocean. When Texas obtained statehood, Polk sought to buy New Mexico and California for fifteen million dollars, but only if Mexico recognized the Rio Grande River as the boundary between the two countries. The Mexican government considered the Nueces River to be the border and refused his offer. The Nueces River is located over one hundred miles from the Rio Grande. This angered Polk, who ordered General Zachary Taylor and four thousand soldiers to cross the Nueces River. When Mexican troops fired on the United States soldiers, Polk asked Congress to declare war on Mexico.

Company K arrived in Point Isabel, Texas, on September 24, 1846. The same day, all the Mexican forces in Monterey, Mexico, surrendered to General Taylor. Jackson spent a frustrating ten months in Port Isabel, located south of Corpus Christi near the mouth of the Rio Grande River, assigned to military post as company supply officer.

During his stay he developed a friendship with another West Point graduate, Lieutenant Daniel H. Hill. One day Jackson asked Hill what it was like to be in a battle. Hill had already seen action in Mexico. Jackson listened intently to what Hill had to say. Then his face lit up and his eyes sparkled as he spoke, "I really envy you men who have been in action . . . I should like to be in one battle."[2]

Vera Cruz

General Winfield Scott, the head of the United States Army, arrived in Mexico shortly after Christmas in 1846 to take command of the United States forces. The following spring Jackson's

company joined Scott's invasion force. Instead of marching his army of fourteen thousand men overland to take the Mexican capital, General Scott chose to move his force by sea.[3] The men, their

Thomas J. Jackson in the uniform he wore during the Mexican War.

equipment, and provisions were ferried down the coast in numerous transport ships. They landed on the beach near the fortress city of Vera Cruz without incident. Jackson later called it "the most thrilling spectacle he had ever seen."[4]

Stationed at Vera Cruz were a small number of Mexican troops. Knowing they were greatly outnumbered and could not expect reinforcements, they eventually negotiated a surrender. Although the battle was short, Jackson finally participated in his first military operation. He also came under fire. A cannonball passed within a few feet of him.

For his "gallant and meritorious conduct" at Vera Cruz, Jackson was promoted to first lieutenant.[5] He was pleased because he felt rank was of the "greatest importance in the army."[6]

Jackson longed for more combat. When he learned that Captain John B. Magruder, a distinguished artillery officer, was forming an independent light artillery unit, he set out to join him. "I wanted to see active service," he said. "To be near the enemy. . . . I knew that if any fighting was to be done Magruder would be at hand."[7]

Magruder, a strict disciplinarian, was hard to please. Few junior officers were interested in serving under him. Jackson easily obtained a position in his unit. Shortly afterward, Magruder's unit joined

General Scott's forces who were advancing on Mexico City.

Contreras and Churubusco

Due to the rough Mexican terrain, Scott chose to approach the city from the south. In his way stood two heavily fortified villages, Contreras and Churubusco. The Mexican troops stationed in these villages controlled all the roadways. Scott assigned his core of engineers, headed by Captain Robert E. Lee, to find a safe route wide enough for his men and artillery to pass through. Lee discovered unmapped trails leading into the Mexican positions that could easily be widened. After being told of Lee's discovery, Scott decided to attack both strongholds simultaneously.

Fighting began on the morning of August 19. Magruder's unit was assigned to create a diversion while the trail was widened. Magruder positioned his guns on a large bluff. The Mexicans battered away at his position with their heavy guns. The shelling went

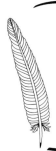

Other graduates of West Point who fought in the Mexican War were: Pierre G. T. Beauregard, Jefferson Davis, Ulysses S. Grant, Joseph E. Johnston, and George B. McClellan.

on for hours. Though heavily outgunned, the Americans maintained their position.

At one point Magruder ordered Jackson to move his two guns into the center of the fighting. Afterward he lost sight of Jackson and thought he had died or been wounded. Later when he moved forward, Jackson joined him, "in handsome style, and kept up the fire with great briskness and effect."[8]

Chapultepec

Two days later the Americans moved around behind the Mexican forces and the battle ended. Now the only Mexican stronghold between the American army and Mexico City was the huge castle of Chapultepec. The castle stood two hundred feet tall and was surrounded by walls three-quarters of a mile long and a quarter of a mile wide. This formidable obstacle housed the Mexican Military Academy.

General Scott decided to destroy the castle by artillery fire. At five o'clock on the morning of September 12, the bombardment began. Jackson was given command of an artillery section and sent to the northern side of the castle. There his section came under heavy enemy fire. His men could not unload their artillery from their caissons (chests which hold ammunition). After many futile efforts, they gave up and hid behind a nearby embankment. Jackson remained with his guns and tried to rally his men by walking back and forth shouting, "There is no danger: see! I am not hit!"[9] Later Jackson admitted that this was the only lie he ever told.

For his bravery at Chapultepec, Jackson received another promotion. He was raised to the temporary rank of major. He also received high praise from his commanders. In an after-action report, Magruder wrote, "upon this occasion, when circumstances placed him in command . . . he proved himself eminently worthy of it."[10] Another commander praised him by reporting, "Lt. Jackson, who, although he lost most of his horses and many of his men, continued chivalrously at his post, combating with noble courage. . . ."[11]

Mexico City

After the battle of Chapultepec, United States forces occupied Mexico City. Jackson was assigned to the occupation forces and spent almost a year housed in the imperial palace and assigned light duties. This gave him time to explore the city he learned to love. "For the mere delight of living, he considered the city of Mexico to surpass all others he had ever known." He also studied Spanish, which he felt was "the natural language of lovers."[12]

Six weeks after being stationed in Mexico City, Jackson hinted in a letter to his sister that he was thinking about staying in Mexico and that he might even marry a lovely Mexican señorita. When his sister fretted about losing her brother, he wrote, "Do not allow my words about marrying in Mexico to disturb you . . . I have no tie in this country equal to you."[13]

In December 1847, twenty-one-year-old Jackson was reassigned to Captain Francis Taylor's company in Mexico City. He renewed his friendship with Taylor, who was the first person to talk seriously with him about religion. A devout Episcopalian, Taylor felt religion was a personal matter. He encouraged Jackson to make a thorough study of religion and find one in which he could believe.

Jackson began his religious quest by investigating the Catholic Church. He visited a community of Catholic monks, and friends arranged for him to meet with the Archbishop of Mexico. He found the Archbishop to be friendly and open to his questions, but he felt a simpler faith would be more to his liking.

Garrison Duty

In 1848 Jackson returned home and was assigned to garrison duty in New York and Pennsylvania forts. During this time he continued to improve his mind by avidly reading. He pursued his interest in history, and read forty or fifty pages a day. In time his eyes began to bother him. Also, his old stomach ailment tormented him again. In order to control his discomfort he resorted to a bland diet consisting of stale whole-grain bread, plainly dressed meats, and simple vegetables such as peas, green beans, or potatoes. He only drank water or strong black tea and exercised for at least three hours per day.

On Sunday, April 29, 1849, Jackson was baptized at St. John's Episcopal Church in New York by Reverend Michael Schofield. Normally when an adult is baptized in church, it means he wishes to join that particular church. Jackson, however, only wanted to officially become a Christian and a Protestant. He would later decide which church most closely matched his faith. In October of 1850, Jackson received orders to report to Florida to help put down the Seminole Indian uprising. While in the middle of a disagreement with his post commander in Florida, he was offered a position at the Virginia Military Institute in Lexington to teach Natural and Experimental Philosophy. His old friend, Major Daniel Harvey Hill, recommended him for the position.

Jackson was eager to leave Florida because he felt his health was suffering. Also, he liked the idea of being closer to his sister and her family. He resigned his commission in the army and accepted the military institute's offer.

5

TROUBLED TIMES

When Thomas Jackson arrived in Lexington, Virginia, in the summer of 1851, most of the townspeople found him hard to get to know. He was painfully shy and never seemed to relax. While sitting down in a chair, he rarely allowed his back to touch the back of the chair nor would he cross his legs. His punctuality became legendary. One could almost tell the time by his rigid adherence to his routine.

Virginia Military Institute

His students at the Virginia Military Institute (VMI) found him to be a difficult and bewildering instructor. He learned each lesson verbatim and repeated it word for word in the order in which he had memorized it. If a cadet asked a question, he would back up and repeat what he said in the same way he had before. He was incapable of explaining anything in simple terms. Many of the cadets thought of him as a multiplication table in pants.[1] They called him "Tom Fool Jackson" and "Square Box" in reference to his enormous feet. Often drawings of his huge feet mysteriously appeared on the blackboard of his classroom.

The Virginia Military Institute was modeled after the United States Military Academy and was called the "West Point of the South."

One of the first friends Jackson made in Lexington was John B. Lyle. He owned a little bookstore on Main Street. The store provided a meeting place for the gentlemen of Lexington who were interested in literature, music, and religion. Lyle, a "courteous, jolly and lovable old bachelor," was a devout Presbyterian.[2] In time, he became Jackson's religious advisor and introduced him to his own pastor, Reverend William S. White. Through Reverend White's guidance, Jackson joined the Presbyterian Church on November 22, 1851. After joining the Presbyterian Church, Jackson's religious activities increased. He taught a Sunday school class made up of elementary school boys and attended prayer meetings every week. When Reverend White scolded his congregation for not coming forward and leading prayer during church services, Jackson felt compelled to volunteer. Due to his shyness, the task turned out to be excruciatingly painful for both Jackson and the congregation. After Jackson's first attempt, Reverend White refrained from asking him to do it again. Finally, Jackson persuaded the Reverend to allow him to try one more time. He wanted to learn how to do it well.

In order to improve his speaking skills, Jackson joined the Franklin Society. The society met regularly on Saturday nights and debated the current political issues of the day. Jackson believed

This portrait of Thomas Jackson is from 1851.

that he could do whatever he willed himself to do, so he forced himself to participate in the society's debates.[3] At first the local newspaper reported him to be a nervous speaker, but in time his delivery improved.

While living in Lexington, Virginia, Jackson renewed his friendship with Major Daniel H. Hill and his wife, Isabella. He frequently visited their home and sometimes escorted Mrs. Hill's younger sisters, Eugenia and Mary Anna Morrision—Anna to her friends and family—when they came to town. The sisters liked Jackson, but they thought his manners were "rather stiff."[4]

Elinor Junkin

Jackson often confided in Major Hill. One day during a visit, he commented that his feeling about a mutual friend—a young lady—greatly confused him. "I don't know what has changed me. I used to think her plain, but her face now seems to me all sweetness."[5]

Hill tried hard to conceal his amusement. "You are in love; that's what is the matter!" he told his friend.[6]

Realizing that Hill was right, Jackson decided he had better do something about it. The young lady in question was Elinor Junkin. Her friends called her Ellie. She was the daughter of Dr. George Junkin, a

Presbyterian minister and president of Washington College. Jackson quickly set out to court her.

Elinor had been born a year later than Jackson, on March 6, 1825. At the age of twenty-eight, she was a devout Christian with a sweet disposition and a talent for drawing. Her older sister and constant companion, Margaret, was a brilliant writer. The two sisters were inseparable. They dressed alike, shared the same room, and did practically everything else together. Prior to meeting Jackson, Elinor showed little interest in the men who called on her.

Jackson did not tell Laura about Elinor, but she might have suspected her brother was in love when she received a letter asking for one of the pictures he had sent her. "It is the smiling one which I want," he told her.[7] He requested that she package it carefully and send it to him by the first possible mail.

The courtship went well for almost three months. Then for some reason Elinor called it off and they went their separate ways. For nearly three months Jackson was beside himself. All he could think about was Elinor. Finally he asked Isabella Hill to intercede for him. Their love triumphed and a wedding date was set. For some unknown reason Elinor insisted that no one be told of their plans. Jackson, who took the promise he made to his future wife literally, did not tell his sister of his plans. This caused a break in their relationship.

On August 4, 1853, in the parlor of the Junkin home on the grounds of Washington University, Thomas Jackson married Elinor Junkin. The private ceremony was performed by Dr. Junkin. The marriage took Lexington by surprise. Not even the Hills had known about the wedding, and Jackson had visited them the morning before the ceremony. This incident illustrated Jackson's ability to keep a secret, for a confidence "could not be blasted out of him!"[8]

Shortly after the ceremony, the couple left on their honeymoon, accompanied by Margaret. They traveled to Philadelphia, West Point, Niagara Falls, Montreal, and Quebec. On their journey back to Lexington they came through Boston and New York. When they returned to Lexington they stayed with the Junkin family and occupied two rooms and the back porch of the house.

Jackson's cadets at Virginia Military Institute would not have recognized their instructor. He thoroughly enjoyed his home life and the congeniality of the Junkin family. For once he was relaxed and happy. Elinor referred to her husband as "The Major" and often teased him. Jackson found his new wife to be a "great source of happiness" for him.[9] Even attending social functions no longer terrified him. As long has he was with Elinor, he was content.

Shortly after returning to Lexington, Jackson began writing to his sister, Laura, again. He sent gifts that he purchased for her and her family while on his honeymoon and told her he was enjoying married life. It took almost a year before Laura forgave her brother for keeping his engagement secret and began writing to him again. Jackson responded by sending her a lock of Elinor's hair and requesting a lock of hers in return. Exchanging locks of hair was a common custom among ladies at the time.

During the winter of 1854, Elinor became pregnant. Concerned for his wife's comfort, he decided they should spend the hot summer months in Beverly, Virginia, where the climate was cooler. Laura was delighted that she would finally meet her new sister-in-law. The visit went well, and Elinor later remarked that she was glad she had gone. But the trip over rough roads took its toll. When they returned to Lexington she immediately took to her bed.

On October 22, 1854, Elinor gave birth to a stillborn daughter. That evening Elinor also died. Two days later cadets from VMI carried Elinor's casket through the snow to the Lexington Presbyterian Cemetery. Jackson's minister, Dr.

White, conducted the funeral services. One of the cadets, Thomas M. Boyd, described how Jackson looked on that sad day. "With cap in his hand he stood beside the open grave. He was extremely pale but calm and resigned. He did not shed a tear, yet everyone who saw him was impressed with the intense agony he was enduring. . . ."[10]

Laura wanted to come to him, but he discouraged her. He continued to live in the Junkin household and bury himself in his normal routine and work. In his notebook he wrote: "Objects to be effected by Ellie's death: To eradicate ambition; to eradicate resentment; to produce humility."[11] Jackson's goal was to get rid of his ambition and anger in order to become more humble.

Sunday School for Slaves

Jackson diligently took on more responsibility in his church. In the autumn of 1855, he organized a Sunday school for slaves. Although Jackson accepted slavery as a fact of life, he felt that slaves should be free and have a chance to lead normal lives. As a Christian he strongly supported the view that slaves should be taught to read, so they could learn from the Bible.

The Sunday school class met every Sunday afternoon promptly at three o'clock. Jackson, the superintendent of the school, began each session with the same song, "Amazing Grace." He did not have an ear for music and this melody was the only tune he could carry. After the song he led a prayer, followed by a Bible story or reading of a passage from the Bible. At this point the class broke up into several small groups and they studied lessons taken from their catechism book. This book summarized the principles of Christianity. The class ended with a closing prayer precisely forty-five minutes after it started. The school was highly successful. Attendance averaged from fifty to a hundred students every week.

At the time, it was illegal to teach slaves to read. Also, in Virginia it was against the law for groups of racially mixed people to meet. Jackson met some opposition to the school from many Virginians who feared another slave rebellion. In 1831 Nat Turner, a religious fanatic, convinced his fellow slaves that he had been chosen by God to lead them to freedom. On August 21, 1831, Turner started an uprising that killed more than fifty whites, including his owner and his owner's family. The rebellion ended three days later, but it took six weeks to capture Turner. He, along with fifteen of his slave followers were tried, convicted, and hanged in Jerusalem, Virginia. As a result of Turner's raid, Southern legislatures imposed stricter rules to control slaves' activities.

Europe

Jackson had planned to spend the summer of 1856 with his sister in Beverly, but at the last minute he changed his mind. He could not stop thinking about Ellie and felt that visiting his sister would only remind him of her. Instead, he set out to tour Europe. On July 9, he sailed for Liverpool, England, on the steamship *Asia*. He visited England, Scotland, Belgium, France, Germany, Switzerland, and Italy before returning to Paris and England and then home. Mainly interested in European culture, he paid little attention to military attractions. The only battlefield he visited was Waterloo, in Belgium near Brussels.

When he returned home, he seemed finally to be able put his grief aside and go on with his life. He delivered a speech at the Franklin Society about his European adventure and started thinking about getting married again. He remembered fondly his visits to the Hill home with Mrs. Hill's sisters,

Information on Jackson's passport described him as: "Stature 5 feet 9 and three-quarter inches, English; forehead full, eyes gray, nose aquiline; mouth small; chin oval; hair dark brown; face oval, complexion dark." At that time he weighed 175 pounds.[12]

Eugenia and Anna. Eugenia was now married, but Anna remained single. Jackson decided to court her. He felt she would be a good companion for him.

Anna Morrision

Anna's first indication of Jackson's intentions came in the form of a letter from him. The communication took Anna completely by surprise. She had never received a letter from Jackson before, and now he was writing to her about the "blissful memories of the summer we had been together in Lexington."[13] Anna did not know what to make of it, but Eugenia did. She predicted that they would soon be seeing Major Jackson.[14]

Jackson's letters continued, and during the Christmas holidays of 1856 he appeared at Anna's home in North Carolina. His leave was short, so he quickly made his intentions known. Anna's hand in marriage was his objective. The Morrison family wanted more time to get to know him, but he pressed them to make a decision before his leave

In an attempt to keep his Sundays free of worldly affairs, Jackson would not write, send, or read a letter on Sunday. He even tried to mail letters so that they would reach their destination before Sunday.

ended. Dr. Morrision was pleased that Jackson was "a Christian gentleman" and a Presbyterian.[15] His wife was charmed by Jackson's "extreme politeness."[16] Anna liked the fact that she and Jackson were already friends and agreed to marry him.

After Jackson's visit the couple communicated for seven months through the mail. On July 16, 1857, they were married in the Morrision home by an old family friend, Dr. Drury Lacy. Anna was a favorite of Dr. Lacy's, and in the ceremony he made Jackson promise to be an "indulgent husband."[17] A few days after the wedding the couple set out on their honeymoon. They visited almost the same places that Jackson had with his first wife.

Since there was a housing shortage in Lexington, the newlyweds stayed in a hotel for a short time, and then lived in boarding houses. They were eager for a house of their own. In a letter to a friend Jackson wrote, "I have taken the first important step by securing a wife capable of making a happy home, and the next thing is to give her an opportunity."[18]

In the winter of 1858, Jackson bought an old two-story brick house on Washington Street in downtown Lexington. The house was in need of repairs and Jackson worked hard to fix it up and make it livable. With simple furnishings Anna made the house homey. Jackson found great happiness in

On July 16, 1857, Thomas Jackson married Anna Morrision.

his home, where there was "a place for everything and everything in its place."[19]

In 1859, Jackson purchased a small farm. The property was located on the edge of town about a mile away from the Jackson home. He enjoyed gardening and grew wheat, corn, and vegetables and planted a small orchard.

At that time Jackson owned a small number of slaves. He acquired Albert and Amy before his marriage. Albert had asked Jackson to purchase him, and then made an agreement with him to work as a hotel waiter to buy back his freedom. Amy, a good cook and housekeeper, appealed to Jackson to buy her when she was being sold to pay a debt. Jackson arranged for her to work for a good Christian family until his marriage, and then she joined his household. Anna brought Heddy, her former nurse, and her two sons with her from North Carolina.

As before, Jackson stringently followed his daily routine. He rose at 6:00 A.M., knelt in prayer, and then took a cold bath. Next he went for a brisk walk no matter what the weather. At 7:00 A.M. he led his family in prayer. He required that everyone in the household attend, and he expected them to be prompt. Anna later recalled that, "he never waited for anyone, not even his wife."[20]

Then breakfast was served and Jackson left for his classes at VMI. He returned at 11:00 A.M. to spend the next two hours in his study standing at a high table reading his Bible and reviewing his lessons for his next day's classes. After lunch he allowed himself half an hour for relaxation.

In the afternoons Jackson worked on his farm or handled other business matters. Before supper he often took Anna for an evening walk or carriage drive. Each evening after dinner he spent an hour mentally studying his lessons for the next day. "He would . . . ask that he not be disturbed by any conversation . . . then take his seat with his face to the wall, and remain in perfect abstraction until he finished his mental task."[21]

That spring, tragedy struck the young couple. On April 30, Anna gave birth to a baby girl. They named her Mary Graham after Anna's mother. The baby was sickly, and on May 22 Jackson wrote to Laura telling her his daughter was "very ill of jaundice."[22] Three days later she died.

Anna grieved over not being able to give her husband a child. He loved children, and it was almost too much to bear to see him dote over other people's little ones. Shortly after their daughter's death, Anna's three-year-old nephew came to live with them. The following October Laura's thirteen-year-old son, Thomas, joined the household so that he could continue his education in Lexington. Jackson enjoyed his fatherly role and playing with the children. He was also a playful and loving husband. At times he would hide behind doors and then spring out and startle Anna with a hug. He liked calling her by Spanish terms of endearment. She was his *esposa* or *esposita* and he was her *esposo*.[23]

John Brown

For several years the Jacksons enjoyed a quiet, happy home life, then the events that lead to the Civil War interfered. The first intrusion came in October of 1859. John Brown, a religious fanatic who wanted to end slavery by any means, attacked the town of Harpers Ferry, West Virginia, and seized the weapons housed in the federal arsenal. Brown needed the weapons to arm the slaves he expected to follow him. His attempt to start a slave rebellion failed. Only five slaves joined him. The next day a group of United States Marines, led by army Lieutenant Colonel

John Brown began his campaign against slavery in Kansas in 1856. His raid on Harpers Ferry was supported by many Northern abolitionists.

Robert E. Lee, stormed the firehouse Brown and his followers had taken and captured them.

Brown was tried and convicted of treason. On November 2, he was sentenced to be hanged in one month. The Governor of Virginia, fearing that Northern abolitionists would try to rescue Brown, requested assistance. Along with the Virginia militia, cadets from the Virginia Military Institute, accompanied by Major Jackson, were sent to Harpers Ferry to help maintain order at Brown's execution. In a letter to Anna, Jackson described the scene:

> John Brown was hung to-day at about half-past eleven . . . Brown had his arms tied behind him, and ascended the scaffold with apparent cheerfulness. . . . The sheriff placed the rope around his neck, then threw a white cap over his head. . . . In this condition he stood for about ten minutes on the trap-door which was supported on one side by hinges and on the other by a rope . . . when the rope was cut by a single blow . . . Brown fell through . . . his knees falling on a level with the position occupied by his feet before the rope was cut. . . . It was an imposing but very solemn scene.[24]

6

WAR AT LAST

After John Brown's raid, tensions continued to build. The sectional differences between the North and the South and the controversy over slavery were leading the nation to war. The Northern economy was based on industry and the Southern economy on agriculture. Slavery died out in the North because of the large number of European immigrants who provided cheap labor in Northern factories. Slavery flourished in the South with the invention of the cotton gin. This simple device used toothed cylinders to pull cotton lint through a wire screen leaving the cotton seed

CREDIT SALE OF A CHOICE GANG OF 41
SLAVES!
COMPRISING MECHANICS, LABORERS, ETC,
FOR THE SETTLEMENT OF A CO-PARTNERSHIP OF RAILROAD CONTRACTORS.

BY J. A. BEARD & MAY, J. A. BEARD, AUCT'R.

WILL BE SOLD AT AUCTION, AT BANKS' ARCADE, MAGAZINE STREET,

ON TUESDAY, FEBRUARY 5th, 1856,
AT 12 O'CLOCK,
A VERY VALUABLE GANG OF SLAVES,

Belonging to a co-partnership, and sold to close the same. The said slaves comprise a gang of 41 choice Negroes. On the list will be found a good Blacksmith, one superior Bricklayer, Field Hands, Laborers, one Tanner, one Cooper, and a first rate woman Cook.

LEWIS, a black man, aged	32	good field hand and laborer.	
SHELLY,	do	26	do	do
PHILIP,	do	30	fair bricklayer.
HENRY,	do	24	fair cooper.
JACOB BATES, do	22	good field hand and laborer.
BOB STAKELEY do	35	do	do
COLUMBUS, do	21	do	do
MARTIN, do	25	do	do
GEORGE, do	30	No. 1 blacksmith.
WESTLY, a griff,	24	a fine tanner and bricklayer.
NELSON, a black man,	30	a good field hand and laborer.
DOCK, do	28	do	do
BIG FRED, do	24	do	do
LITTLE SOL, do	22	do	do
ALFRED, a griff,	28	do	do
SIMON, a black man,	21	do	do
WATT, do	30	do	do
JIM LEAVY, do	24	do	do
JIM ALLEN, do	26	do	do
FRANK GETTYS, a griff,	26	do	do
JERRY GETTYS, a black,	23	do	do
BILL GETTYS, do	23	do	do
GRANDERSON, do	24	do	do
LITTLE FED, do	23	do	do
FRANK HENRY, a griff,	23	do	do
EDMOND, do	21	do	do
ANDERSON, a black man,	24	a No. 1 bricklayer and mason.
BOB SPRIGS, a griff,	25	a good field hand and laborer.
ELIJAH, a black man,	35	do	do
JACK, do	30	do	do
REUBEN, do	28	unsound.
STEPHEN, do	22	a good field hand and laborer.
YELLOW JERRY, a griff,	28	a good teamster.
BIG SOL, a black man,	26	a good field hand and laborer.
BILL COLLINS. do	28	do	do
JESS, do	26	do	do
JUDGE, do	30	do	do
JERRY CARTER, do	28	do	do

LOUISA, a griff, 38 years, a good Cook and seamstress, and an excellent servant.
ROBERT, 13 years old, defect in one toe.
JASPAR, 24 years old, an extra No. 1 laborer, driver and coachman.
The slaves can be seen four days previous to the day of sale. They are fully garantied against the vices and maladies prescribed by law, and are all selected slaves.

TERMS OF SALE—One year's credit for approved city acceptances or endorsed paper, with interest at 7 per cent. from date, and mortgage on the slaves if required
ACTS OF SALE BEFORE WM. SHANNON, NOTARY PUBLIC, AT THE EXPENSE OF THE PURCHASERS.

After the sale of the above list of Slaves, will be sold Another lot of Negroes, comprising Field Hands, House servants and Mechanics. A full description of the same will be given at the sale. The slaves can be seen two days previous to the sale.

This banner was used to advertise slaves for sale.

behind. By hand, a slave could produce about one pound of cotton lint per day. By using the cotton gin, a slave could produce three hundred to one thousand pounds per day.[1] Over the years, the demand for cotton soared until the South's economy depended on slavery.

Many Northerners believed slavery was a horrible sin. They felt it was wrong for one person to own another. They were called abolitionists and tried to prevent the spread of slavery into new territories acquired by the United States. At first compromises were made, but in time many Southerners became increasingly uneasy about staying in the Union. They talked about withdrawing from the Union and forming their own government.

Jackson did not believe that his home state of Virginia would leave the Union. In a letter to Laura he wrote that he was "strong for the Union . . . and if things become no worse I hope to continue so. I think the majority in this country are for the Union, but in counties bordering on us there is a strong secession feeling."[2]

A month later he wrote to his nephew, Thomas Arnold, and stated his views on secession. He was in favor of making a "thorough trial for peace" and for Virginia to do everything possible to maintain the Union, but if her rights were denied, he favored secession. He also cautioned his young namesake about war, "People who are anxious to bring on war don't know what they are bargaining for; they don't see all the horrors that must accompany such an event."[3]

Election of 1860

The last straw in the conflict was the presidential election of 1860. Jackson belonged to the Democratic party, as did many Southerners. Prior to the election the party split, and each section nominated its own presidential candidate. Jackson supported the candidacy of John C. Breckinridge of Kentucky, the Southern candidate. The Northern candidate was Stephen Douglas of Illinois. John Bell of Tennessee ran for the presidency on the Constitutional Union ticket.

Due to the party split, no single Democratic candidate could obtain enough votes to be elected. The Republican candidate, Abraham Lincoln, won the election. He received 40 percent of the votes from the Northern states but made a poor showing in the South. In seven Southern states he did not receive a single vote.[4]

The South rebelled. Shortly after the presidential election, South Carolina seceded from the Union. In the next two months, six more states—Mississippi, Florida, Alabama, Georgia,

Louisiana, and Texas—joined her. On February 8, 1861, they formed the Confederate States of America. A provisional government was established in Montgomery, Alabama. The Confederacy also adopted a Constitution similar to the United States Constitution but added provisions for states' rights and slavery.

When Lincoln won the election, there were thirty-three states in the Union. By the time he took office, only twenty-seven remained. In his inaugural address, he declared secession to be illegal and made an eloquent plea for Americans not to destroy "our national fabric, with all its benefits, its memories, and its hopes."[5] He also made it clear that he would do everything in his power to "hold, occupy and possess" any United States property held within the Confederacy.[6]

Lincoln was referring to Fort Sumter in the harbor of Charleston, South Carolina. Sixty-eight men under the command of Major Robert Anderson were trapped more than four months, due to the controversy over whom the fort belonged to—the North or the South. They were cut off from reinforcements and surrounded by six thousand militia from South Carolina and their artillery batteries. Finally, Lincoln took a stand and informed the Confederacy that he intended to send provisions to the fort. After midnight on April 12, the

The Confederate flag flies over Fort Sumter on April 19, 1861, the day after it was taken by Confederate forces.

Confederate War Department sent representatives to talk with Major Anderson. He was informed that if he did not surrender in four hours, the South Carolina troops would open fire. He refused and the first confrontation of the Civil War began. Anderson held out for thirty-four hours and then surrendered. Miraculously, the only one killed during the bombardment was a horse.

After the fall of Fort Sumter, Lincoln issued a call to raise seventy-five thousand volunteers to serve in the United States Army. Their task was to carry out the laws of the Union and put down the rebellion. Governor John Letcher of Virginia would not allow his state's forces to be used in such a manner. On April 17, Virginia seceded from the Union and joined the Confederacy.

Jackson had no doubts about his loyalties. First and foremost, he was a Virginian. When the Virginia Military Institute received orders to send their corps of cadets to Richmond, Jackson accompanied them as their commander.

The orders arrived early on the morning of Sunday, April 21, 1861. The cadets were ordered to be ready for inspection at 10:00 A.M., eat lunch at noon, and then march out at 12:30 P.M. Jackson asked his minister, Reverend White, to come to the barracks and say a prayer before they left. The cadets finished their meal and prayers ahead of time and urged Jackson to get started. Always punctual he replied, "When the clock strikes the hour we will march, and not until then."[7] He sat on his camp stool in front of the barracks and waited. At 12:25 P.M. he requested the roll be called. At exactly 12:30 P.M., he rose from his seat and ordered the cadets to, "Right face! By file, left march!"[8]

After Jackson had delivered the corps of cadets to Richmond, he found himself temporarily without orders. With no official duties, he volunteered his services as drillmaster. On April 25, he was appointed to the rank of major in the Virginia Engineering Corps. This was a disappointment, for

In May of 1861, the Confederate Congress moved their capital from Montgomery, Alabama, to Richmond, Virginia. They expected most of the fighting to take place in the border states, and they wanted their capital to be nearby.

it was the same rank he had held as a professor at the Virginia Military Institute.

A few of his influential friends in Richmond became aware of his predicament and lobbied to have his assignment changed. In a short time his name was withdrawn from the staff assignment and he was commissioned a colonel in the Virginia Army. When his name was put before the Secession Convention to confirm his rank, one of the delegates asked, "Who is Major Jackson . . .?"[9] A delegate familiar with Jackson replied, "He is the one who, if you order him to hold a post, will never leave it alive to be occupied by the enemy."[10]

Harpers Ferry

After receiving his appointment, Jackson was given command of Harpers Ferry. Strategically located on the border between the North and the South, Harpers Ferry was the key to protecting the fertile Shenandoah Valley of Virginia. Jackson's orders were to take charge of the volunteers who had assembled there and to ship all the guns and arms-making machinery in the town to Richmond as soon as possible.

In a letter to Anna, Jackson expressed how pleased he was with his assignment. "I am very much gratified with my command, and would rather have this post than any other in the State."[11] He was also pleased when he learned that Robert E. Lee had been appointed commander and chief of the Virginia forces. "I regard him as a better officer than General Scott," he told her.[12]

On April 29, Jackson arrived at Harpers Ferry. His command consisted of forty-five hundred undisciplined Virginians. The raw recruits needed to

Robert E. Lee and Thomas Jackson had a lot in common. They both graduated from West Point and served in the Mexican War. After the Mexican War, Lee became the superintendent at West Point and Jackson a professor at the Virginia Military Institute. Although they certainly knew of each other, their first documented meeting was in January 1854, when Jackson visited West Point with his first wife, Ellie. After their visit, Lee wrote a letter of recommendation for a position Jackson applied for, but never received, at the University of Virginia. Both men were in Harpers Ferry for the hanging of John Brown.

Robert E. Lee was offered the field command of the United States Army when the Civil War began. He declined and resigned his commission. Then he joined the Confederate Army and was given command of the Army of Northern Virginia.

learn how to function as a unit and become proficient in the use of their weapons. He quickly began a rigorous program to transform them into soldiers. At five o'clock each morning they were awakened by the sound of bugles. The first thing they did was drill, followed by drill, drill, and a little more drill. They practiced marching, using their weapons, and following commands. Between drills they would stop for roll call or to eat.

Many of the new soldiers thought Jackson was crazy because of his obsession with drilling. Also, he did not look or act like the typical army officer. He went about his duties wearing "the plain blue" uniform of the Military Institute. No gold lace or insignia marked him as a high-ranking officer. "His well-worn cadet cap was always tilted over his eyes; he was sparing in speech; his voice was very quiet, and he seldom smiled."[13] He did not speak often "even to his officers" and confided in no one.[14]

Hunter McGuire was one of the volunteers who came to Harpers Ferry to enlist. A young-looking twenty-five-year-old, McGuire studied medicine in his hometown of Winchester and at Jefferson Medical College in Philadelphia. Shortly after he arrived in Harpers Ferry, he received a commission as a surgeon in the Army of the Shenandoah and was appointed medical director. When he reported to Jackson, his commanding officer, he was told to go to his quarters and wait for further instructions. A week later his orders were posted. When McGuire got to know Jackson better, he asked why his orders had been delayed. Jackson told him he looked so young, that he personally wrote to Richmond to make sure a mistake had not been made.

Anna wrote suggesting that she join him at Harpers Ferry. Jackson was convinced that Virginia would be in the middle of war soon and wrote back saying he would be delighted to see her but for her not to come. Since their nephews had returned to their homes, he advised her to close up their house in Lexington, Virginia, and join her family in North Carolina. A dutiful wife, she followed his instructions and placed their servants in good homes before she left.

Jackson acquired his favorite horse shortly after taking command of Harpers Ferry. Jackson's men had seized five carloads of cattle and horses. One of the animals caught Jackson's eye—a small, stocky, sorrel (brownish-orange-colored) horse. He thought the mild-mannered animal would make a good mount for Anna. Later he decided to keep the horse for himself and named him Fancy. His men renamed the horse Little Sorrel. Like his owner, Little Sorrel possessed a great deal of endurance. During resting periods he had the habit of lying down like a dog, and Jackson, who loved fruit, would feed him apples. Jackson rode him almost every day and often napped while in the saddle.[15]

While in Harpers Ferry, Jackson became acquainted with a colorful cavalry officer, James Ewell Brown Stuart. His friends called him Jeb. He graduated from West Point in 1854. When Virginia seceded from the Union, he resigned his commission in the United States Army and joined the Confederacy. He was commissioned a colonel in the 1st Virginia Cavalry and took command of a troop of three hundred horsemen.

Stuart was a flamboyant dresser. He wore a Confederate-gray coat lined in red silk, tiny golden spurs on his knee-high boots, and an ostrich feather stuck in the top of his brown felt hat. His sword was hooked in a gold silk sash around his waist, and he wore white buckskin gloves. Despite his appearance and good-humored personality, Stuart took his command seriously. He would not send his troopers anywhere he would not go himself. He religiously followed orders and was an officer Jackson could depend on.

On May 15, Jackson was relieved of his command at Harpers Ferry by Brigadier General Joseph E. Johnston. Forty-four-year-old Johnston had an extensive military career. He was the highest-ranking United States Army officer to resign his commission and join the Confederacy. Three days after losing his command, Jackson wrote to Anna.

James Ewell Brown (Jeb) Stuart was known for his bold raids and reconnaissance—information gathering missions.

He feared she might be upset when she heard the news. "My Precious darling," he wrote, "I suppose you have heard that General Joseph E. Johnston, of the Confederate army, has been placed in command here. You must not concern yourself about the change . . . I hope to have more time, as I am not in command of a post, to write longer letters to my darling pet."[16]

When fresh troops arrived in the middle of June, Johnston reorganized his forces at Harpers Ferry into four brigades. Jackson was given command of the First Brigade, which consisted of the 2nd, 4th, 5th, 27th, and 33rd Virginia Regiments. Also attached to Jackson's command was the Rockbridge Artillery. William Nelson Pendelton, an Episcopal rector who oversaw his parish, commanded the unit composed of twenty-eight college graduates, twenty-five seminary students, and seven men who held master's degrees from the University of Virginia.

The First Brigade was basically a young unit, whose members ranged from eighteen to twenty-five years of age. The youngest member of the First Brigade was supposedly fifteen and the oldest sixty. Two-thirds of the men were farmers, blacksmiths, masons, or machinists. One brigade member estimated that "not more than one out of thirty of the members owned slaves."[17] Many of the men were related to each other. A lot of the companies were composed of fathers, sons, brothers, uncles, and cousins.

Johnston felt that Harpers Ferry was impossible to defend against the Union forces that were building up around him. "We are about leaving this place," Jackson wrote his wife on June 14. "General Johnston has withdrawn his troops from the Heights (Maryland and Virginia), has blown up and burnt the railroad bridge across the Potomac, and is doing the same with respect to the public buildings."[18]

Due to its strategic location, Harpers Ferry continually shifted hands between the North and the South during the Civil War.

The following day Johnston's entire army marched out of Harpers Ferry toward Winchester. As they withdrew they destroyed everything that could be useful to the Union Army. Jackson's men burned the railroad buildings at Martinsburg, including forty-two locomotives and over three hundred railroad cars. Many of the railroad cars were filled with coal and burned for weeks. It "was a sad work," Jackson wrote his wife, "but I had my orders, and my duty was to obey."[19]

Falling Waters

Johnston left Jackson's brigade and Stuart's horsemen at Camp Stevens near Martinsburg. Their orders were to observe the Union Army and to fall back if they advanced in large numbers. On the morning of July 2, Stuart informed Jackson that the Union troops were advancing from about four miles away. Jackson left two of his regiments to stand by as reserves and took one regiment, about three hundred fifty men, and one piece of artillery to meet the Union advance.

Near a church called Falling Waters, five miles south of the Potomac River, Jackson placed his men in the fields and waited. He intended to provoke a confrontation in order to determine the strength of the Union forces. When the Union troops appeared, they walked into a hail of musket fire. Then Jackson's men charged.

In a short time Jackson realized his men were severely outnumbered. He ordered them to fall back but to continue fighting. For the next three hours they accomplished the difficult task of keeping their formation, halting, firing, and then falling back. They withdrew nearly three miles under enemy fire.

During the battle a cannonball ripped through a tree near where Jackson was standing writing a message. Pieces of the tree scattered around him, but he did not move an inch and continued to write.

While the infantry withdrew, Jeb Stuart's cavalry closed off the roads on both sides of the Union Army. In the process he captured two Union officers and forty-seven enlisted men. At this point the Union forces settled into Martinsburg and advanced no farther. The Confederate losses at the end of the battle were thirteen men killed or missing and twelve wounded. The Union losses were six dead, eighteen wounded, and one missing.[20]

General Johnston praised Jackson for the way he handled the skirmish at Falling Waters and recommended him for a promotion. On July 3, General Lee wrote to Jackson, "My dear general, I have the pleasure of sending you a commission of brigadier-general in the Provisional Army, and to feel that you merit it. May your advancement increase your usefulness to the State."[21]

Lee relied heavily on Jackson. He could always count on him to follow his orders willingly and without question. Jackson once said he would follow Lee "blindfolded because he was so cautious."[22]

Jackson was pleased with his promotion and proud of his men. Two weeks later, in the first Battle of Manassas, they fought valiantly against tremendous odds and turned the battle around. Afterward Jackson became known as "Stonewall," and his troops the "Stonewall Brigade." They were one of the boldest and most feared fighting units of the whole war. Devoted to "Old Jack," as they called him, they would attempt the impossible whenever he requested it.

7

THE BATTLEFIELD

After the first battle of Manassas, the Confederate Army spread out over northern Virginia to wait for the next Union attack. Jackson and his men camped near Centreville and then the Fairfax Court House. Many times rumors of enemy movements were reported, but the Union forces never materialized.

On October 13, 1861, Jackson was promoted to the rank of major general and assigned to command the Confederate forces in the Shenandoah Valley. This meant leaving his beloved brigade. On the chilly afternoon of November 4, he rode out to say good-bye to his assembled troops. "Officers and men of the First Brigade, I am not here to make a speech, but simply to say farewell. I first met you at Harpers Ferry at the commencement of the war, and I cannot take leave of you without giving expression to my admiration of your conduct from that day to this. . . ."[1]

Jackson paused and stood up in his stirrups. Then he raised his hand to his men and with a high-pitched voice continued. "In the Army of the Shenandoah, you were the First Brigade! In the Army of the Potomac you were the First Brigade! In the Second Corps of this army you were the First Brigade! You are the first Brigade in the affections of your general. . . . Farewell!"[2]

The men cheered again and again. Jackson waved his cap in response and rode off toward Winchester, over twenty-five miles away, where he would establish his new headquarters.

Valley Campaign

When Jackson arrived in Winchester, he was appalled by the defenselessness of the Valley and the lack of experienced soldiers. He immediately telegraphed Richmond for reinforcements and made a special request. He wanted his old brigade to join him. General Johnston prized the First Brigade and protested their removal from his command. The

War Department compensated Johnston by sending him twice the number of men he was losing.

Jackson took his new command seriously. He knew that the Valley was a natural avenue of invasion for the Union Army. He believed that if the Shenandoah Valley was lost, so was Virginia. He vigorously trained his troops and made plans for a winter assault.

On New Year's Day, 1862, Jackson's troops plus six thousand men under the command of General William L. Loring marched out of Winchester. His goal was to take Romney, forty miles away in western Virginia, and sever the communication link between the Union armies in Maryland and western Virginia. He also wanted access to the rich farmland in the southern branch of the Valley to help feed his men.

It was an unusually warm winter's day, and many of the men stored their tents, blankets, and coats in the supply wagons that followed them. By noon the weather shifted and it began to rain. By nightfall the rain turned to sleet and the temperature dropped to zero. Because of the weather, the supply wagons fell behind and could not reach the men until morning. They spent the night, hungry and cold, in the middle of a blizzard.

During the night, one member of the Stonewall Brigade rolled over on the cold ground to face his

General Thomas "Stonewall" Jackson and his staff.

campfire and shouted, "I wish the Yankees was in hell!"[3]

"I don't," replied the man next to him, "for if they were, Old Jack would be within half a mile of them, with the Stonewall Brigade in front."[4]

A bystander later told Jackson about the conversation. He reportedly broke out in a hearty laugh—something he rarely did. Jackson depended on the Stonewall Brigade. He gave them the hardest assignments, so the other brigades in his command would not think he favored them.[5]

After fourteen days of marching through the snow-covered mountains, Jackson and his men captured Romney. In a letter to his family, one soldier wrote, "When we marched into town every soldier's clothing was a solid cake of ice, and icicles two inches long were hanging from the hair and whiskers of every man."[6]

After a few days, Jackson left General Loring's troops in charge of Romney and returned to Winchester. Unhappy with their assignment and Jackson's leadership, Loring and his men petitioned Richmond for permission to return to Winchester. When permission was granted and they returned to Romney, Jackson was furious. He wrote to the Confederate secretary of war and requested orders to return to the Virginia Military Institute or that he be allowed to resign his commission. "With such interference in my command," he wrote, "I cannot expect to be of much service in the field."[7]

John Letcher, the governor of Virginia, and General Johnston persuaded Jackson to withdraw his resignation. When General Loring and his men were removed from the Valley, he agreed to stay.

Shortly after Jackson returned to his quarters in Winchester, Anna joined him for the winter. They stayed with the family of Reverend James Graham and called it their "war home."[8] She later recalled that it was one of the most pleasant times of their lives together. "We spent as happy a winter as ever falls to the lot of mortals on earth."[9] During her three-month stay in Winchester, Anna became pregnant again. In March, when it appeared the Union Army was preparing for another assault, Jackson sent Anna home to North Carolina. They would not see each other again for thirteen months.

On February 26, 1862, Union General Nathaniel P. Banks left Maryland with forty thousand men and set out to take the Shenandoah Valley. Once he had achieved his goal, he was ordered to join the main part of the Union Army in Virginia for the assault on Richmond.

Jackson was instructed to protect the Shenandoah Valley and prevent Banks's troops from leaving. At the time, his command consisted of only four thousand five hundred men. Although sorely outnumbered, nine to one, he set out on a fast-moving Valley Campaign that thoroughly confused the Union leadership. His secret, quick marches became legendary. His men never knew where they were going until they got there. Often he would be seen riding up and down the marching line encouraging his men to close up their lines and push on. On May 23, they marched twenty-six miles in sixteen hours, earning them the title of "foot cavalry."[10]

Jackson's Valley Campaign illustrated two of his rules for military success. "Always mystify, mislead, and surprise the enemy if possible; and when you strike and overcome him never let up in pursuit so long as your men have strength to follow."[11]

His other rule was:

> Never fight against heavy odds, if by any possible maneuvering you can hurl your own force on only a part—and that the weakest part—of your enemy and crush it. Such tactics will win every time, and a small army may thus destroy a large one in detail; and repeated victory will make it invincible.[12]

Another key to Jackson's success in the Valley was the addition of Jedediah Hotchkiss to his staff. Hotchkiss, a thirty-three-year-old former school-teacher, was fascinated with engineering and cartography—map making. When he volunteered his services, Jackson gave him an assignment. "I want you to make me a map of the valley, from Harper's Ferry to Lexington, showing all the points of offence and defence in those places."[13]

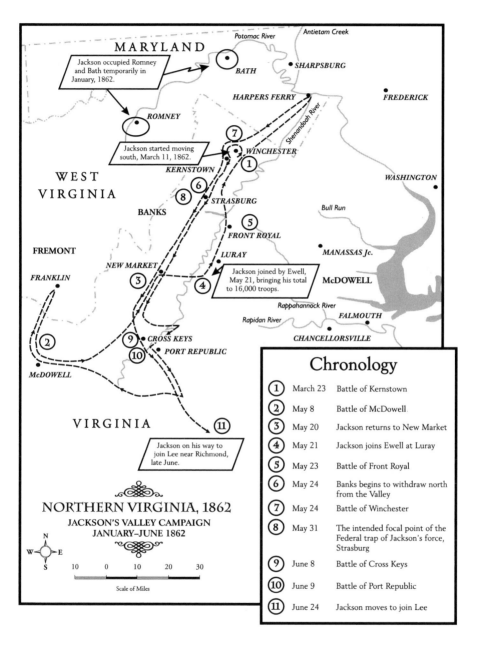

MARYLAND

Potomac River   Antietam Creek

Jackson occupied Romney
and Bath temporarily in
January, 1862.

• BATH   • SHARPSBURG

HARPERS FERRY   • FREDERICK

ROMNEY

⑦

Jackson started moving
south, March 11, 1862.

• WINCHESTER

WEST   KERNSTOWN   ①   WASHINGTON

VIRGINIA   ⑥

⑧   • STRASBURG

BANKS   Bull Run

⑤

FRONT ROYAL

FREMONT   LURAY   • MANASSAS Jc.

FRANKLIN   NEW MARKET   Jackson joined by Ewell,
May 21, bringing his total
to 16,000 troops.   McDOWELL

③   ④

Rappahannock River

Rapidan River   FALMOUTH

⑨ • CROSS KEYS   CHANCELLORSVILLE

⑩ • PORT REPUBLIC

McDOWELL

VIRGINIA   ⑪

Jackson on his way to
join Lee near Richmond,
late June.

NORTHERN VIRGINIA, 1862

JACKSON'S VALLEY CAMPAIGN
JANUARY–JUNE 1862

N
W ✦ E
S   10   0   10   20   30

Scale of Miles

Chronology

①	March 23	Battle of Kernstown
②	May 8	Battle of McDowell
③	May 20	Jackson returns to New Market
④	May 21	Jackson joins Ewell at Luray
⑤	May 23	Battle of Front Royal
⑥	May 24	Banks begins to withdraw north from the Valley
⑦	May 24	Battle of Winchester
⑧	May 31	The intended focal point of the Federal trap of Jackson's force, Strasburg
⑨	June 8	Battle of Cross Keys
⑩	June 9	Battle of Port Republic
⑪	June 24	Jackson moves to join Lee

This map shows the route Jackson took on his Valley Campaign in 1862.

Equipped with notebooks, a compass, and an altimeter—an instrument for determining elevation, Hotchkiss set out to prepare sketches that he would later use to draw Jackson's maps. He explored Manassanuteen Mountain and documented a route around the mountain that enabled Jackson to move his troops easily from one side of the Valley to the other. This information was the key to his fast-moving attacks and quick disappearances.

By the end of the Valley Campaign, Jackson immobilized sixty thousand Union soldiers and frightened Washington politicians into thinking their city would soon be under attack. This led to the withdrawal of part of the Union Army in Virginia to protect Washington. Jackson's tactics ensured the safety of the Valley and captured a large supply of badly needed arms and supplies for the Confederate Army.

Regarding the Valley Campaign, Jackson remarked, "He who does not see the hand of God in this is *blind*, sir, blind!"[14] He believed in providence and felt a battle was won because it was God's will.

In Defense of Richmond

Despite the withdrawal of part of the Union Army, General George B. McClellan, the commander of the Army of the Potomac, was camped only nine miles outside Richmond with one hundred thousand

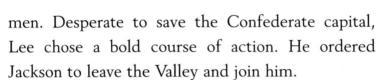

Richmond became the key to military planning for both sides during the war. The main objective of the Union Army was to take Richmond, and the main objective of the Confederate Army was to protect it.

men. Desperate to save the Confederate capital, Lee chose a bold course of action. He ordered Jackson to leave the Valley and join him.

Lee's plan was to take the initiative and instead of waiting for McClellan to make another move, attack from the west while Jackson's forces attacked from the northwest. In the middle of the afternoon of June 26, the Confederate forces attacked the Union Army at Mechanicsville. They met strong resistance and were repeatedly beaten back. At nightfall they moved out of range of the Union artillery.

Although General McClellan telegraphed Washington proclaiming victory, he was worried about the overwhelming size of the Confederate Army. He had received reports from the Pinkerton Detective Agency that Lee's army consisted of two hundred thousand men. Actually Lee's forces were less than half that size, but McClellan was sure the reports were correct. Otherwise Lee would not have divided his army. Also, McClellan was worried that Jackson would soon cut him off from his supply line. He decided to move his home base southward down the peninsula, on the James River, to Harrison's Landing.

As the Union Army backed up the peninsula, the Confederate troops followed. Battles were waged at Gaines' Mill, Savage's Station, Frayser's Farm, and Malvern Hill. Lack of adequate food and rest hindered the Confederate Army's performance in what became known as the Seven Days Battle. Compounded with confusing orders, bad weather, and unfamiliar terrain, they won only one battle.

Due to stress and exhaustion, Jackson made the worst showing of his entire military career. Prior to the battles, he spent fourteen hours riding to attend a meeting with Lee in Richmond on June 23. The next day he turned around and, with little rest or food, rode back to join his troops. Then Jackson failed to arrive at the battle of Mechanicsville when he was expected and was late in reaching the field at Gaines' Mill. He also showed an uncharacteristic lack of initiative during the battle of Frayser's Farm.

Later Jackson admitted that he had not been well during the week of the Seven Days Battles. He claimed that he had suffered from "fever and debility."[15]

During the seven days of fighting, both armies lost a large number of men. The casualty count—number

The Pinkerton National Detective Agency was founded by Allen Pinkerton in 1850. During the Civil War the agency ran a spy ring behind Confederate lines. Disguised as Major E. J. Allen, Pinkerton supplied exaggerated reports about the size of the Confederate troops to General McClellan, due to faulty sources.

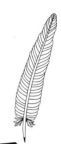

of men killed, wounded, captured, or missing—was sixteen thousand for the Confederate Army and twenty thousand for the Union Army.

Second Battle of Manassas

On July 2, McClellan finally reached the safety of the Union gunboats in Harrison's Landing. His officers urged him to mount a counterattack. He refused. Then Lincoln turned to General John Pope, who was forming a new Union force called the Army of Virginia.

Pope was not a popular man. His pompous ways offended his officers and Southerners hated him.[16] He threatened to hang, without a trial, anyone he suspected of aiding the Confederacy and permitted his men to seize food and supplies from Virginia farms without paying for them.

Lee considered Pope to be an evil man who needed to be stopped.[17] He divided his army into two commands and sent Jackson to engage Pope.

The first battle took place at Cedar Mountain, Virginia, on August 9. Two weeks later, in order to move around and behind Pope's army, Jackson took his twenty-five thousand troops over a fifty-six-mile march around the right side of Pope's army. Within two days he severed Pope's connection to the Washington railroad and looted his supply depot in Manassas Junction. One of Jackson's men had fond memories of that afternoon.

> It makes an old soldier's mouth water now just to think of it. Some filled their haversacks with cakes, some with candy, others with oranges, lemons, canned goods. . . . I know one that took nothing but French mustard; it turned out to be the best thing taken, as he traded it for bread and meat. . . .[18]

Jackson decided not to wait for Pope at Manassas Junction. He moved on and securely established his men on a ridge overlooking the Manassas battlefield—the same battlefield where he had defeated the Union Army the year before and earned his nickname, "Stonewall."

Pope declared that he would "bag the whole crowd" and attacked on August 29. Jackson's men again held their ground.[19] When ammunition started to run out, the Confederate soldiers threw rocks. Pope, confident Jackson's army would retreat, planned to pursue them the next day. Instead, Jackson received reinforcements. Five divisions under the command of Major General James

Longstreet attacked Pope's army along a two-mile front. Pope's forces were beaten back.

Out of seventy thousand men, Pope lost nearly fifteen thousand. Between Jackson's and Longstreet's divisions there were fifty-five thousand men, and they lost approximately ten thousand. Shortly after the second Battle of Manassas, President Lincoln sent Pope to Minnesota to put down an Indian uprising. Then he turned command of all the Union forces back to General McClellan.

Maryland

Once again Lee needed to relieve the pressure on Richmond. He did not have the military strength to take on the Union forces surrounding Washington, so he decided to move his army north into Maryland. By winning a battle in Union territory he hoped to frighten the North into ending the war in favor of the South. Also, he wanted to gain European recognition. If England and France recognized the Confederacy, he felt they would try to break the Union blockade of Southern ports.

When Lee crossed the Potomac into Maryland, he knew that many Marylanders sympathized with the South, and he hoped they would join him and rebel against the Union. He instructed his men to sing "Maryland, My Maryland" as they marched along. The people of Maryland greatly disappointed him, for they stayed behind their closed doors and watched.

One Maryland woman thought Lee's men were "the dirtiest" soldiers she had ever seen.[20] Another woman, observing from her doorstep, later wrote:

> This body of men moving . . . along with no order, their guns carried in every fashion, no two dressed alike, their officers hardly distinguishable from the privates . . . were these . . . the men that had . . . driven back again and again our splendid legions?[21]

On September 10, Lee sent Jackson's army to eliminate the Union garrison at Harpers Ferry. This would secure his communication line between Richmond and the Shenandoah Valley.

McClellan pursued Lee's army, and by a quirk of fate, acquired a copy of the Confederate orders for the Maryland campaign. In a meadow where the Confederates had previously camped, a Union corporal found the orders written on a piece of paper wrapped around three cigars. Worried it might be a trap, McClellan proceeded cautiously and waited sixteen hours before advancing on Lee's army. By that time, nineteen thousand Confederates had positioned themselves on the crest of a four-mile ridge east of Sharpsburg, Maryland, at a creek called Antietam.

On September 15, McClellan's army of ninety-five thousand men began to approach the town. Still cautious, he spent two days preparing for battle.

Finally he attacked on September 17, which would be remembered as the "bloodiest single day of the war."[22] The two armies fought head-on throughout the day. The Union forces outnumbered the Confederates, more than two to one, but they chose to attack piecemeal—in stages. Each time they attacked, the Confederates were able to hold their ground. At one point the Confederate line almost gave way, but reinforcements arrived just in time. It was a bloodbath. Both sides suffered tremendous losses. The dead or dying covered the battlefield. The Union casualties were 2,108 soldiers killed

Dead Confederate soldiers lay by a fence on Hagerstown Road on the Antietam battlefield.

and another 10,302 wounded or missing. The Confederate losses were 2,700 men killed, 9,024 men wounded, and about 2,000 missing. McClellan lost a sixth of his army, and Lee lost a fourth.

If McClellan had not hesitated again and attacked the next day, he might have destroyed the Confederate Army. Instead he waited, which permitted Lee to escape back across the Potomac. McClellan followed Lee's army but too far away to engage him.

Shortly after Jackson returned to Virginia, he learned that his daughter had been born on November 23, 1862. His sister-in-law, Harriet Irwin, wrote a letter pretending to be the baby. "I am a very tiny little thing. I weigh only eight and a half pounds . . . My aunts both say that I am a little beauty. My hair is dark and long, my eyes are blue . . ." The letter was signed "Your Dear little wee Daughter."[23]

Jackson had wanted a boy for he felt that "men have a larger sphere of usefulness than women."[24] But he immediately wrote to his sister-in-law and asked her to, "give the baby a shower of kisses from her father, and tell her that he loves her better than all the baby-boys in the world, and more than all the other babies in the world."[25]

At Jackson's request, Anna named the baby after his mother, Julia. "My mother was mindful of me when I was a helpless, father-less child, and I wish to commemorate her now."[26] They chose Laura, after Jackson's sister, for the child's middle name.

Fredericksburg

President Lincoln was infuriated with General McClellan's reluctance to engage the Confederate Army after the battle of Antietam. He replaced McClellan with General Ambrose E. Burnside. Knowing he needed to take action quickly, Burnside moved his army into the hills on the outskirts of Fredericksburg, Virginia. He planned to cross the Rappahannock River, take Fredericksburg, and then move on to Richmond.

Since the bridges at Fredericksburg no longer existed, Burnside waited seventeen days for a pontoon bridge to arrive to take his one hundred twenty thousand men across the river. This delay gave the Confederate Army time to evacuate the town and entrench their seventy-five thousand soldiers in the hills surrounding Fredericksburg. Jackson's position was to cover the right of the Confederate battle line while Longstreet's men covered the left.

The Union assault began at ten o'clock on the morning of December 13. Just as the sun broke through the fog, the Union soldiers advanced. It was a glorious sight. One eye-witness later said:

The fluttering flags, the long lines of glittering bayonets, the well-dressed officers, the prancing horses, the roll of drums, the notes of the bugles . . . it was more like a holiday parade than . . . any day of real battle.[27]

Longstreet jokingly asked Jackson if the massive Union forces frightened him. Jackson replied, "We shall see very soon whether I shall not frighten them."[28]

Jackson appeared that morning in a new dress coat, a gift from Jeb Stuart. Stuart had it specially made for Jackson by a Richmond tailor. About the same time, Anna sent him a new cap that was

A view of Fredericksburg from across the Rappahannock River in February of 1863.

covered with gold braid. For once Jackson actually looked like a general. Many of his men did not like it. They were fearful that without his old, rumpled uniform their "Old Jack would be afraid of [soiling] his clothes and would not get down to his work."[29] They need not have worried, for Jackson was as fierce as ever.

The battle of Fredericksburg raged until sundown. At one point Jackson's battle line was penetrated, but his artillery quickly forced the Union soldiers back. On Marye's Heights, Longstreet's men continuously shot down the advancing Union soldiers. Brigade after brigade fell before the Union soldiers reached the Confederate line.

Burnside wanted to renew the battle the next day, but his staff talked him out of it. He kept his army in position until the evening of December 15, when under the cover of fog, they withdrew across the Rappahannock River. Burnside paid mightily for his folly. Union casualties totaled 12,700 men out of a force of 122,000. Confederate losses were 5,300 out of 72,500.

General Lee thought that Burnside might cross over the Rappahannock River again and sent Stuart's cavalry to investigate. He reported some activity at Port Royal, but when Jackson's army arrived it turned out to be a rumor. Heading back toward

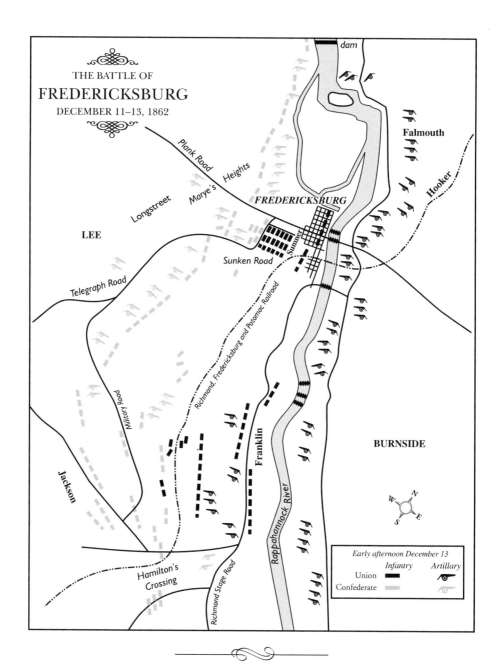

THE BATTLE OF
FREDERICKSBURG
DECEMBER 11–13, 1862

Plank Road

Heights

Marye's

Longstreet

FREDERICKSBURG

Falmouth

Hooker

LEE

Sunken Road

Sumner

Telegraph Road

Richmond, Fredericksburg and Potomac Railroad

Military Road

Franklin

BURNSIDE

Jackson

Rappahannock River

N
W   E
S

Early afternoon December 13
Infantry   Artillary
Union
Confederate

Hamilton's
Crossing

Richmond Stage Road

dam

On December 13, 1862, the Union troops tried to storm the Confederate
Army in a brave but hopeless attack at Fredericksburg, Virginia.

Fredericksburg, they camped out in the woods near a large mansion called Moss Neck. The Corbin family owned the house and invited Jackson and his staff to stay with them.

At first Jackson refused for he found their house "too luxurious for a soldier, who should sleep in a tent."[30] He camped out in the woods about five hundred yards away. When the weather grew colder, he relented and set up his headquarters in a small house on the Corbin property that had been used as an office. Jackson's men built themselves log houses in the woods nearby.

A frequent visitor to Jackson's headquarters was five-year-old Janie Corbin. She took a liking to Jackson and spent many an afternoon playing on the floor beside him while he worked. He always tried to have a piece of candy or fruit to give her. One day he took out his pocketknife and cut away the gold braid from the hat Anna had given him. Then he wrapped it around Janie's head like a crown.[31]

In March, Jackson moved his headquarters to Hamilton's Crossing. Shortly afterward, he learned that Janie had come down with scarlet fever and died. The news brought tears to his eyes.[32] He sent a staff member to console the Corbin family, and carpenters from the Stonewall Brigade made Janie's coffin.[33]

While at Hamilton's Crossing, Jackson sent for Anna and the baby. He found housing for them in the home of William Yerby. On April 20 in the middle of a rainstorm, they arrived by train. Jackson's overcoat was dripping wet when he greeted them but his face was "aglow with happiness."[34] Little Julia smiled at him and could not be taken out of his arms until they arrived at their lodging. They spent nine wonderful days together before the war interfered.

8

HIS LAST BATTLE

The Confederate and Union Armies sat across the Rappahannock River watching each other, waiting for spring to come. Sometimes they shouted good-naturedly across the river. A few times they even rowed out in small boats to trade tobacco, coffee, or newspapers.

One day, Jackson came down to the river accompanied by a group of officers and ladies. The Union soldiers tipped their hats to the ladies who graciously waved their handkerchiefs in reply. Then General Jackson took out his binoculars and coolly surveyed them. One Union soldier later wrote, "we could have shot him with a revolver," but there was an agreement that neither side would fire.[1]

The winter break ended on April 29, 1863, when the Union Army, under the command of General Joseph Hooker, moved to attack Lee's forces. President Lincoln instructed General Hooker to destroy Lee's army. Hooker conceived a simple strategy to achieve this goal. He planned to attack the Confederate front at Fredericksburg while the main part of his army marched up the Rappahannock River, crossed, and attacked Lee's forces from the rear. He hoped this would force Lee to retreat to Richmond across the Union front lines where he could easily destroy them.

The Union forces reached Chancellorsville on April 30. Chancellorsville was not a town, just a crossroads where several roads intersected. Nearby, a single house stood in a clearing surrounded by a thick forest called the Wilderness. General Hooker and his staff moved into the downstairs of the Chancellor House and continued to plan their assault to trap Lee's forces.

The Union maneuvers did not fool General Lee. Even though he was outnumbered more than two to one, he divided his army to meet the Union advance at Chancellorsville. When the Confederate troops arrived at the edge of the forest, the Union troops engaged them in battle. For some unknown reason,

A painting by E.B.D. Julio of Lee and Jackson's last meeting.

General Hooker ordered his men back into positions near the Chancellor House shortly after the battle began.

That evening Lee and Jackson met. Puzzled by the Union's retreat Lee asked, "How can we get at these people?"[2] Jackson replied it was up to Lee to decide. He would do whatever his commander thought best. Lee examined a map for a few moments. He reasoned that his army had to take the initiative, so he came up with a daring plan. He would send Jackson to attack Hooker's forces from the rear near Chancellorsville. General Stuart's cavalry would cover Jackson's movements.

After coming up with the plan, Lee asked Jackson how he would proceed. "With my whole corps," he replied.[3]

Lee had not expected this answer. "What will you leave me?" he asked.[4]

Jackson replied he would leave two divisions. This meant that Lee would only have fourteen thousand men to hold off Hooker's force of fifty thousand. The boldness of Jackson's plan inspired Lee. "Well," he replied, "go on."[5]

A local guide was found who knew of a secluded road that was wide enough to accommodate artillery. At five o'clock the following morning, Jackson and his corps of twenty-eight thousand men

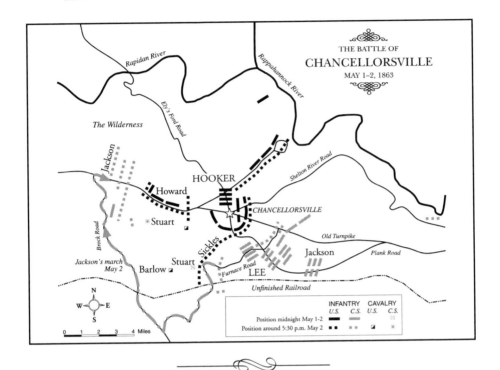

Jackson's men completed a fast march around the right flank of the Union Army during the battle of Chancellorsville in Virginia.

started their twelve-mile hike through the Wilderness around the Union's right flank.

Jackson ordered, "See that the column is kept closed and that there is no straggling."[6] He kept encouraging his men by saying, "Press forward."[7]

Their movements did not go unnoticed. There were numerous reports from Union pickets that a large group of Confederates was moving on the roads west, but Hooker convinced himself that Jackson was retreating.

Two hours before sunset on May 2, Hooker's

soldiers were making coffee and playing cards. Their guns were stacked out of reach. Suddenly, deer came running out of the forest followed by Jackson's men. Coming from every direction and yelling loudly, they attacked. Hooker's men, caught completely off guard, panicked and ran. By sunset they had fallen back nearly two miles.

Wounded

Jackson, eager to continue the battle, rode out to scout for a night attack. In the dark, nervous Confederates fired on his party, killing two of his aides. Jackson was hit once in the right hand and twice in his left arm. Little Sorrel, his horse, bolted.

The officers accompanying Jackson helped him off his horse and sat him under a nearby tree. They examined his wounds and tried to stop the bleeding. Jackson was in a great deal of pain, but a doctor could not be found. They placed him on a stretcher and carried him across the battlefield. Fearful that the men would lose their courage if they knew General Jackson was wounded, the officers hovered over him. When asked, they just said they were helping a friend. From the litter Jackson whispered to them, "Just say it is a Confederate officer."[8]

It was almost midnight when Jackson reached the field hospital and the care of his old friend, Dr. McGuire. After examining Jackson's shattered left

This photograph was taken of Thomas Jackson two weeks before he was wounded in the Battle of Chancellorsville.

arm, McGuire informed him that it would have to be amputated and asked if he could proceed. Jackson replied that he should do whatever he thought best.[9]

Hundreds of soldiers lost an arm or leg during the Civil War. Since there were no antibiotics to help fight gangrene, physicians felt it was safer to remove a limb than risk infection.

When awakened in the middle of the night and told that General Jackson was wounded and his arm amputated, General Lee remarked, "He has lost his left arm, but I have lost my right."[10] Lee knew he needed Jackson as much as he needed his own right hand.

Over the next few days, Jackson's condition seemed to improve. He had many visitors and often asked about the progress of the battle. When told of the courage of his men, he remarked that someday they would be proud to tell their children that they were members of the Stonewall Brigade. Then he added that the name Stonewall "belongs to the brigade and not to me."[11]

Lee was fearful for Jackson's safety. He ordered Jackson's hospital tent be guarded both day and night. Finally he insisted that Jackson be moved to a safer location and that Dr. McGuire accompany him.

Guiney's Station

Jackson was taken to the home of friends, the Chandler family, at Guiney's Station twenty-seven miles away.

He asked his brother-in-law to go to Richmond and bring his wife and daughter to him at the Chandlers' home. Anna had gone to Richmond the month before, after visiting her husband at Hamilton's Crossing.

Shortly before his wife arrived, his condition worsened. He awoke in the night with a severe pain in his right side. He had developed pneumonia, probably due to a cold he had caught while sleeping outdoors.

On Sunday, May 10, Dr. McGuire informed Anna Jackson that her husband would not live out the day. Anna gently told her husband this. At first he did not believe her. Then he asked Dr. McGuire if it was so. After Dr. McGuire confirmed what Anna told him, he seemed to accept it. He said it was good. "I always wanted to die on Sunday."[12]

Throughout the rest of the day he was delirious, going in and out of consciousness. Shortly after three that afternoon, he said, "Let us cross over the river, and rest under the shade of the trees."[13] Then he died.

After his death Jackson's staff officers dressed him in civilian clothes and a blue military coat.[14] This coat was possibly the one Jeb Stuart had given him. His uniform was unusable. It was torn and bloody. Then they placed him in a coffin and laid sprigs of flowers around his head. His open casket was placed in the parlor of the Chandler House.

9

EPILOGUE

Late that afternoon, General Lee telegraphed the following message to the Confederate secretary of war. "It becomes my melancholy duty to announce to you the death of General Jackson. He expired at 3:15 P.M. today. His body will be conveyed to Richmond in the train tomorrow. . . ."[1]

The Stonewall Brigade petitioned General Lee to allow them to accompany Jackson's body. He refused their request by saying that not even he could leave his post long enough to bid farewell to Jackson, for "those people over the river are again showing signs of movement."[2] Then he added that Jackson always did his duty and would not have approved of his old brigade leaving their post to bury him.[3]

A special railroad car was sent to Guiney's Station to carry Jackson's body to Richmond. During the forty-five mile trip, the train was detained at almost every railroad station by crowds of mourners. At Ashland, Virginia, fifteen miles north of the Confederate capital, a group of women boarded the train to place fresh flowers and wreaths on the general's coffin.

In Richmond, businesses closed and flags flew at half-mast. Five thousand people waited at the train station in the stifling heat. When the train finally arrived, Jackson's coffin was placed in a hearse drawn by two white horses and taken to the large reception room in the executive mansion.

That night Jackson's body was embalmed. Sculptor Frederick Volck and his assistant Pietro Zamboggi made a plaster death mask of his face. Then his body was placed in a metal casket.

The next day a formal procession carried Jackson's casket through the city to the Confederate House of Representatives. His casket was placed on a white-draped altar in front of the speaker's bench and covered with the Confederate flag.

More than twenty thousand people came to say farewell to their general. Late that evening, guards tried to close the doors but were shouted down by the crowd still waiting to get in. One old man yelled while waving his empty sleeve, "I give my arm for him, damn ye, and I'm agoing to see him, too!"[4] Officials decided to leave the doors open until everyone who wanted to pay their respects to Jackson could file by.

The next day, Wednesday, May 13, Jackson's casket was placed on a train bound for Lexington. At every stop people gathered to give Anna flowers and wreaths. Many times they asked to see "Stonewall Jackson's baby!"[5]

Jackson's casket arrived in Lexington late Thursday evening and was immediately taken by the cadets from the Virginia Military Institute to Jackson's old lecture room. Every half hour until sunset, cadets outside saluted Jackson with their artillery. A pair of cadets guarded his coffin through the night.

Friday morning, Jackson's funeral service was held at the Presbyterian Church where he had been a deacon. Jackson's old pastor, Reverend White, officiated at the service. Reverend White's simple eulogy was followed by a brief service, and then the hymn, "How Blest the Righteous When He Dies" was sung. A Bible reading from First Corinthians was followed by a sermon. After the service, Jackson's coffin was taken to the Presbyterian Cemetery—now the Stonewall Jackson Memorial Cemetery—and he was laid to rest.

Anna Jackson never remarried. She moved to North Carolina to be near her family and wrote a book about her husband. She was often honored by Confederate veterans and their families. In 1890 she received a widow's pension of twenty dollars a month for her husband's participation in the Mexican War. Previously, she refused a pension from the state of North Carolina. She died on March 24, 1915.

Jackson's daughter, Julia, married William Edmond Christian, a Richmond newspaperman, in 1885.

Mourners gather around Jackson's grave in Lexington, Virginia.

Shortly after Jackson's death, the area surrounding his boyhood home and birthplace chose to separate from the Confederate state of Virginia and join the Union. The people of western Virginia had strong ties to the Union and many of them disapproved of slavery. That area became the State of West Virginia.

They had two children, Julia and Thomas. She died at the age of twenty-seven in 1889.

Stonewall Jackson's sister, Laura Jackson Arnold, divorced her husband, Jonathan, in 1870. During the war she nursed Union soldiers and was regarded as, "an angel of mercy among the sick."[6] After the war she refused to allow anyone to call her brother "Stonewall." It took Anna Jackson over a year to get a letter to her sister-in-law informing her of Jackson's death. The letter also contained a lock of Jackson's hair.

Jackson's favorite horse, Little Sorrel, lived to be over thirty years old. After the war, Anna Jackson kept him on the family farm in Lincoln County, North Carolina. When he died, she had him stuffed and given to the Virginia Military Institute.

Dr. Hunter McGuire joined General Lee's staff as medical director after Jackson's death. When the war was over, he became the chief of surgery at the

Medical College of Virginia. In 1892 he was elected president of the American Medical Association. He died at the age of eighty in 1900.

After Jackson was wounded at Chancellorsville, Jeb Stuart led his troops to victory. A year and a day after Jackson's death, Stuart was mortally wounded in the Battle of Yellow Tavern near Richmond. He was taken to Richmond and lingered for a day in extreme pain. He died on May 12 and was buried in the Hollywood Cemetery.

Two months after Lee lost Jackson, he undertook a disastrous campaign in Gettysburg, Pennsylvania, that many historians feel was the turning point in the Civil War. From then on the Union Army successfully beat back the Confederate troops until Lee surrendered at Appomattox Courthouse in Virginia almost two years later.

On May 30, Jackson's brigade was officially designated the "Stonewall Brigade" by the secretary

When the statue honoring Jackson was built in 1891, his body was removed from the burial site and his remains examined. It was noted that his clothes were still in good condition, but his coat was blue. At that time, people had difficulty accepting the fact that a Confederate general, who should have been wearing a gray coat, was buried in a blue one.

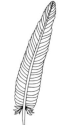

of war. It was the only large unit in the Confederate Army to have its nickname formally recognized. They carried their name with pride for the remainder of the war. When Lee surrendered at Appomattox, there were 210 members of the Stonewall Brigade still alive. Over the course of the war, approximately five thousand men served in the brigade.[7]

Some claim that if Jackson had lived, the Civil War would have ended differently. Even Lee felt that if Stonewall Jackson had been at Gettysburg, the battle would have ended in a total victory, and the independence of the Confederacy would have been established.[8]

In 1891 the survivors of the Stonewall Brigade paid their final tribute to their general. They joined almost thirty thousand people who came to Lexington for the dedication of a statue of Jackson that was placed at his graveside. The members of the brigade decided they wanted to spend one more night with their general, so they camped out in the cemetery. The townspeople found them huddled around Jackson's statue covered in blankets and overcoats. Concerned for their health, they tried to persuade the old soldiers to come inside. One of the old men rose and explained that many times they had slept around "Old Jack" in the battlefield, and they wanted to sleep near him one more time.[9]

CHRONOLOGY

1824—Born in Clarksburg, Virginia.

1826—Sister, Elizabeth, dies on March 5. Father, Jonathan Jackson, dies on March 26.

1831—Mother, Judith Jackson Woodson, dies on December 3.

1841—Brother, Warren, dies in November.

1842—Attends the United States Military Academy at West Point. -1846

1847—Fights in Mexican War. -1848

1848—Returns to the United States and is stationed at Fort Hamilton.

1850—Transferred to Fort Meade.

1851—Resigns his commission in the army and joins the staff of the Virginia Military Institute (VMI).

1853—Marries Elinor Junkin on August 4.

1854—Elinor gives birth to a stillborn child and dies on October 22.

1856—Tours Europe.

1857—Marries Mary Anna Morrison on July 16.

1858—Daughter Mary Graham born on April 30 and dies on May 25.

1861—Accompanies cadets from VMI to Harpers Ferry; Given command of Harpers Ferry on April 29; Earns the nickname "Stonewall" at the First Battle of Bull Run on July 21; Assigned command of Confederate forces in the Shenandoah Valley on November 4.

1862—Carries out Valley Campaign; Seven Days Battle fought June 25 through July 2; Second Battle of Bull Run fought August 27 through 30; Battle of Antietam on September 17; Daughter Julia born on November 23; Battle of Fredericksburg on December 13; Establishes winter quarters at Moss Neck on December 16.

1863—Wounded in Battle of Chancellorsville on May 2; Dies on May 10.

CHAPTER NOTES

Chapter 1

1. Geoffrey C. Ward, *The Civil War: An Illustrated History* (New York: Alfred A. Knopf, 1990), p. 62.

2. Time-Life Books, *Spies, Scouts, and Raiders* (Alexandria, Va.: Time-Life Books, 1985), p. 26.

3. Ibid., p. 23.

4. Katharine M. Jones, *Heroines of Dixie* (New York: Bobbs-Merrill Co., Inc., 1955), pp. 61–62.

5. R. L. Dabney, *Life and Campaigns of Lieutenant-General Thomas J. Jackson* (New York: Blelock & Co., 1866), p. 212.

6. George F. R. Henderson, *Stonewall Jackson and the American Civil War* (New York: Longmans, Green, and Co., 1932), vol. 1, p. 147.

7. Byron Farwell, *Stonewall: A Biography of General Thomas J. Jackson* (New York: W. W. Norton & Company, 1992), p. 179.

8. James I. Robertson, Jr., *The Stonewall Brigade* (Baton Rouge, La.: Louisiana State University Press, 1963), p. 39.

9. Henderson, p. 145.

10. Ibid., p. 150.

11. Ibid.

12. Robertson, p. 41.

13. Dabney, p. 223.

14. Thomas L. Livermore, *Numbers & Losses in the Civil War in America: 1861–65* (Bloomington, Ind.: Indiana University Press, 1957), p. 77.

15. Lenior Chambers, *Stonewall Jackson: The Legend and the Man* (New York: William Morrow & Company, Inc., 1959), vol. 1, p. 392.

16. Farwell, p. 194.

17. Joy Hakim, *War, Terrible War* (New York: Oxford University Press, 1994), p. 69.

18. Ibid.

Chapter 2

1. Frank E. Vandiver, *Mighty Stonewall* (New York: McGraw-Hill Book Company, Inc., 1957), p. 6.

2. Roy Bird Cook, *The Family and Early Life of Stonewall Jackson* (Richmond: Old Dominion Press, Inc., 1925), p. 44.

3. Ibid., p. 45.

4. Paul D. Casdorph, *Lee and Jackson: Confederate Chieftains* (New York: Paragon House, 1992), p 22.

5. Vandiver, p. 10.

Chapter 3

1. Roy Bird Cook, *The Family and Early Life of Stonewall Jackson* (Richmond: Old Dominion Press, Inc., 1925), p. 71.

2. Frank E. Vandiver, *Mighty Stonewall* (New York: McGraw-Hill Book Company, Inc., 1957), p. 13.

3. Ibid.

4. Lenior Chambers, *Stonewall Jackson: The Legend and the Man* (New York: William Morrow & Company, Inc., 1959), vol. 1, p. 53.

5. John Bowers, *Stonewall Jackson: A Portrait of a Soldier* (New York: William Morrow & Company, Inc., 1989), p. 54.

6. Byron Farwell, *Stonewall: A Biography of General Thomas J. Jackson* (New York: W. W. Norton & Company, 1992), p. 18.

7. Paul D. Casdorph, *Lee and Jackson: Confederate Chieftains* (New York: Paragon House, 1992), pp. 44–45.

8. Vandiver, pp. 16–17.

9. Farwell, p. 25.

10. Vandiver, p. 17.

11. Ibid., p. 18.

12. Bowers, p. 223.

13. Casdorph, p. 47.

Chapter 4

1. Don Nardo, *The Mexican-American War* (San Diego: Lucent Books, 1991), p. 18.

2. Burke Davis, *They Called Him Stonewall* (New York: Rinehart & Company, Inc., 1954), p. 97.

3. Nardo, p. 66.

4. Byron Farwell, *Stonewall: A Biography of General Thomas J. Jackson* (New York: W. W. Norton & Co., 1992), p. 44.

5. Davis, p. 97.

6. Frank E. Vandiver, *Mighty Stonewall* (New York: McGraw-Hill Book Company, Inc., 1957), p. 30.

7. Davis, p. 100.

8. Ibid., p. 103.

9. George F. R. Henderson, *Stonewall Jackson and the American Civil War* (New York: Longmans, Green, and Co., 1932), vol. 1, p. 41.

10. Farwell, p. 56.

11. Elihu S. Riley, *Stonewall Jackson: A Thesaurus of Anecdotes of and Incidents in the Life of Lieut-General Thomas Jonathan Jackson* (Annapolis, Md.: Riley's Historic Series, 1920), p. 13.

12. James I. Robertson, Jr., "Stonewall Jackson: Molding the Man and Making a General," *Blue & Gray Magazine*, June 1992, p. 12.

13. Davis, p. 106.

Chapter 5

1. Burke Davis, *They Called Him Stonewall* (New York: Holt, Rinehart & Winston, Inc., 1954), p. 115.

2. Byron Farwell, *Stonewall: A Biography of General Thomas J. Jackson* (New York: W. W. Norton & Co., 1992), p. 103.

3. Davis, p. 115.

4. Elihu S. Riley, *Stonewall Jackson: A Thesaurus of Anecdotes of and Incidents in the Life of Lieut-General Thomas Jonathan Jackson* (Annapolis, Md.: Riley's Historic Series, 1920), p. 45.

5. Farwell, p. 110.

6. Lenior Chambers, *Stonewall Jackson: The Legend and the Man* (New York: William Morrow & Company, Inc., 1959), vol. 1, p. 248.

7. Frank E. Vandiver, *Mighty Stonewall* (New York: McGraw-Hill Book Company, Inc., 1957), p. 91.

8. Ibid., p. 96.

9. Ibid., p. 100.

10. Farwell, p. 117.

11. Chambers, p. 260.

12. Davis, pp. 120–121.

13. Chambers, p. 275.

14. Vandiver, p. 112.

15. Chambers, p. 275.

16. Ibid.

17. Vandiver, p. 115.

18. Ibid., p. 117.

19. Ibid.

20. George F. R. Henderson, *Stonewall Jackson and the American Civil War* (New York: Longmans, Green, and Co., 1932), vol. 1, p. 68.

21. Davis, pp. 126–127.

22. Farwell, p. 131.

23. Davis, p. 129.

24. Mary Anna Jackson, *Memoirs of Stonewall Jackson* (Louisville, Ky.: The Prentice Press Co., 1895), pp. 130–131.

Chapter 6

1. Geoffrey C. Ward, *The Civil War: An Illustrated History* (New York: Alfred A. Knopf, 1994), p. 12.

2. Burke Davis, *They Called Him Stonewall* (New York: Holt, Rinehart & Winston, Inc., 1954), p. 132.

3. Frank E. Vandiver, *Mighty Stonewall* (New York: McGraw-Hill Book Company, Inc., 1957), p. 128.

4. Paul D. Casdorph, *Lee and Jackson: Confederate Chieftains* (New York: Paragon House, 1992), p. 155.

5. Byron Farwell, *Stonewall: A Biography of General Thomas J. Jackson* (New York: W. W. Norton & Co., 1992), p. 144.

6. Richard M. Ketchum, *American Heritage Picture History of the Civil War* (New York: American Heritage Publishing Co., 1960), p. 59.

7. Farrell, p. 149.

8. Vandiver, p. 132.

9. Lenior Chambers, *Stonewall Jackson: The Legend and the Man* (New York: William Morrow & Company, Inc., 1959), vol. 1, p. 317.

10. Ibid.

11. Ibid.

12. Vandiver, p. 134.

13. George F. R. Henderson, *Stonewall Jackson and the American Civil War* (New York: Longmans, Green, and Co., 1932), vol. 1, p. 115.

14. Ibid., pp. 114–116.

15. Davis, p. 16.

16. Mary Anna Jackson, *Memoirs of Stonewall Jackson* (Louisville, Ky.: The Prentice Press Co., 1895), pp. 157–158.

17. James I. Robertson, Jr., *The Stonewall Brigade* (Baton Rouge, La.: Louisiana State University Press, 1963), p. viii.

18. Jackson, pp.160–161.

19. Chambers, p. 349.

20. Ibid., p. 353.

21. Ibid., p. 354.

22. Casdorph, p. 387.

Chapter 7

1. Elihu S. Riley, *Stonewall Jackson: A Thesaurus of Anecdotes of and Incidents in the Life of Lieut-General Thomas Jonathan Jackson* (Annapolis, Md.: Riley's Historic Series, 1920), pp. 117–118.

2. Ibid.

3. James I. Robertson, Jr., *The Stonewall Brigade* (Baton Rouge, La.: Louisiana State University Press, 1963), p. 59.

4. Ibid.

5. Ibid., p. viii.

6. Ibid., p. 62.

7. Frank E. Vandiver, *Mighty Stonewall* (New York: McGraw-Hill Book Company, Inc., 1957), p. 192.

8. Mary Anna Jackson, *Memoirs of Stonewall Jackson* (Louisville, Ky.: The Prentice Press Co., 1895), p. 213.

9. Vandiver, p. 191.

10. Robertson, p. 90.

11. Riley, p. 7.

12. Ibid.

13. Jed Hotchkiss, *Make Me a Map of the Valley* (Dallas: Southern Methodist University Press, 1973), p. 10.

14. Geoffrey C. Ward, *The Civil War: An Illustrated History* (New York: Alfred A. Knopf, 1994), p. 138.

15. Vandiver, p. 327.

16. Ward, p.146.

17. Ibid.

18. Ibid., p. 147.

19. Ibid.

20. Ibid., p. 151.

21. Richard Wheeler, *Voices of the Civil War* (New York: NAL Dutton, 1990), p. 181.

22. Ward, p. 160.

23. Paul D. Casdorph, *Lee and Jackson: Confederate Chieftains* (New York: Paragon House, 1992), p. 348.

24. Byron Farwell, *Stonewall: A Biography of General Thomas J. Jackson* (New York: W.W. Norton & Co., 1992), p. 455.

25. Vandiver, p. 419

26. Jackson, p. 19.

27. Farwell, p. 472.

28. John Bowers, *Stonewall Jackson: A Portrait of a Soldier* (New York: William Morrow & Company, Inc., 1989), p. 313.

29. Wheeler, p. 215.

30. Vandiver, p. 436.

31. Lenior Chambers, *Stonewall Jackson: The Legend and the Man* (New York: William Morrow & Company, Inc., 1959), vol. 2, p. 339.

32. Ibid.

33. Ibid., pp. 339–340.

34. Casdorph, p. 376.

Chapter 8

1. Elisha Hunt Rhodes, *All for the Union* (Lincoln, R.I.: Wowbry, 1985), p. 104.

2. Douglas Freeman, *Lee: An Abridgement in One Volume*, Richard Harwell, ed. (New York: Charles Scribner's Sons, 1961), p. 291.

3. Ibid., p. 292.

4. Ibid.

5. Ibid.

6. Frank E. Vandiver, *Mighty Stonewall* (New York: McGraw-Hill Book Company, Inc., 1957), p. 469.

7. Ibid.

8. Ibid., p. 480.

9. Ibid., p. 484.

10. Freeman, p. 302.

11. George F. R. Henderson, *Stonewall Jackson and the American Civil War* (New York: Longmans, Green, and Co.,1932), vol. 2, p. 462.

12. Burke Davis, *They Called Him Stonewall* (New York: Holt, Rinehart & Winston, Inc., 1954), p. 445.

13. Ibid., p. 446.

14. Lenior Chambers, *Stonewall Jackson: The Legend and the Man* (New York: William Morrow & Company, Inc., 1959), vol. 2, p. 449.

Chapter 9

1. Byron Farwell, *Stonewall: A Biography of General Thomas J. Jackson* (New York: W. W. Norton & Co., 1992), p. 527.

2. Ibid., p. 528.

3. Ibid.

4. Burke Davis, *They Called Him Stonewall* (New York: Holt, Rinehart & Winston, Inc., 1954), p. 450.

5. Ibid., p. 451.

6. Farwell, p. 531.

7. James I. Robertson, Jr., *The Stonewall Brigade* (Baton Rouge, La.: Louisiana State University Press, 1963), p. viii.

8. Paul D. Casdorph, *Lee and Jackson: Confederate Chieftains* (New York: Paragon House, 1992), p. 397.

9. Robertson, p. 246.

GLOSSARY

ambush—A surprise attack.

antibiotics—Medication used in the prevention and treatment of infectious diseases.

artillery—The branch of the army specializing in the use of heavy mounted guns.

battalion—A military unit composed of a headquarters and two or more units.

bayonet —A knife attached to the top of a rifle and used as a weapon in close combat.

brigade—A military unit consisting of a variable number of men organized for a specific purpose.

cavalry—Troops trained to fight on horseback.

Confederacy—The Southern states that seceded from the United States in 1860 and 1861.

engage—To enter into conflict with.

flank—The right or left side of a military formation.

furlough—A leave of absence.

garrison—A permanently established military post.

infantry—Soldiers trained, armed, and equipped to fight on foot.

litter—A device for carrying a sick or injured person; a stretcher.

Manifest Destiny—The nineteenth-century doctrine that the United States had the right and duty to expand throughout the North American continent.

outflank—To outmaneuver or outwit.

picket—A detachment of soldiers on guard duty.

quartermaster—An officer responsible for obtaining food, clothing, and equipment for troops.

regiment—A military unit of ground troops consisting of at least two battalions.

secede—To formally withdraw from membership.

Union—The United States of America regarded as a national unit, especially during the Civil War.

FURTHER READING

Boatner, Mark M., III. *The Civil War Dictionary*. New York: Vintage Books, 1991.

Casdorph, Paul D. *Lee and Jackson: Confederate Chieftains*. New York: Paragon House, 1992.

Civil War Society. *The American Civil War: A Multicultural Encyclopedia*. Danbury, CT: Grolier Education Corporation, 1994.

Davis, Burke. *They Called Him Stonewall*. New York: Holt, Rinehart & Winston, Inc., 1954.

Freeman, Douglas S. *Lee: An Abridgement in One Volume*, Richard Harwell, ed. New York: Charles Scribner's Sons, 1961.

Fritz, Jean. *Stonewall*. New York: Putnam, 1979.

Hakim, Joy. *War, Terrible War*. New York: Oxford University Press, 1994.

Kent, Zachary. *The Civil War: "A House Divided."* Springfield, NJ: Enslow Publishers, Inc., 1994.

Nardo, Don. *The Mexican-American War*. San Diego: Lucent Books, 1991.

Robertson, James I., Jr. *The Stonewall Brigade*. Baton Rouge, LA: Louisiana State University Press, 1963.

Tate, Allen. *Stonewall Jackson: The Good Soldier*. Ann Arbor: Ann Arbor Paperbacks, 1957.

Ward, Geoffrey. *The Civil War: An Illustrated History*. New York: Alfred A. Knopf, 1994.

INDEX